CW00358143

Welcome to
BLETCHLEY PARK

Bletchley Park has global significance. It is where the World War Two Codebreakers broke seemingly impenetrable codes and ciphers, and it is where the world's first electronic computers were installed and operated.

The intelligence produced here contributed to all theatres of World War Two. Bletchley Park pioneered co-operation with other intelligence services including France, Poland and the United States. The techniques developed here played a major role in the Cold War and, in many cases, remain highly relevant today.

The site is a portal into the information age in which we live, as unique data-processing machines were developed to help speed up the codebreaking effort.

Bletchley History 1938 to now

In 1938 the British Government bought part of the then much larger Bletchley Park estate to house the most secret codebreaking and intelligence efforts of the Government Code and Cypher School (GC&CS) in a quiet rural location, easily reached from London, Cambridge and Oxford. It was fully expected that in a future war London would come under heavy air attack. Over the next few months, as war loomed, the first wooden huts were built and communications channels were established. GC&CS finally moved from London in August 1939.

Early in the war the Bletchley Park operation centred on the work of a small group of experts. It went on to pioneer the application of close inter-service liaison and production line methods to the key stages of the process – collection, codebreaking, evaluation and dissemination.

German Air Force and Army Enigma settings were changed daily at midnight and even before the first Enigma ciphers were broken in early 1940, Cambridge mathematician Gordon Welchman realised GC&CS would need a structured, factory-like process to ensure the daily settings were broken as efficiently as possible. In April 1940, after the invasion of Norway, a round-the-clock shift system was introduced.

From May 1940 there was a massive increase in the volume and complexity of traffic, as the theatre of war widened. The so-called Phoney War ended with the German invasion of Denmark and Norway in April 1940. A new Enigma key was introduced and it took the Codebreakers in Hut 6 six days to break it. This break into the new key told the Allies every move the German Army was making, and was about to make.

Captain Ridley's
Shooting Party 1938

By early 1943 Bletchley Park had developed from a small community of specialist cryptanalysts into a vast and complex global signals intelligence factory. It hit its peak in early 1945, when around ten thousand people worked at Bletchley and its associated outstations. The contributions of Bletchley Park's Codebreakers to the outcome of World War Two are now globally recognised. They include:

- Location of the German 'U-Boat' submarines in the Battle of the Atlantic
- Providing early warning of German air attacks on British cities
- Production of intelligence to support the Mediterranean and North African campaigns
- Contributing to the success of Operation Overlord through the work of a number of sections at Bletchley Park in breaking German High Command, military and Secret Service communications, as well as Japanese diplomatic messages
- Helping to identify new weapons including German V weapons, jet aircraft, atomic research and new U-Boats
- Analysis of the effect of the war on the German economy
- Breaking Japanese codes and producing intelligence that helped secure the successful outcome of the war in the Pacific

After the war, GC&CS became Government Communications Headquarters (GCHQ) and it left Bletchley Park in 1946. The site was used as a training school for the Control Commission which governed post-war Germany, then a teacher training college, and later a training centre for the Civil Aviation Authority and the GPO, which became British Telecom. In 1992 a group of local historians saved the site from developers' bulldozers and the Bletchley Park Trust was formed to preserve the site for the nation.

The same view of The Mansion today

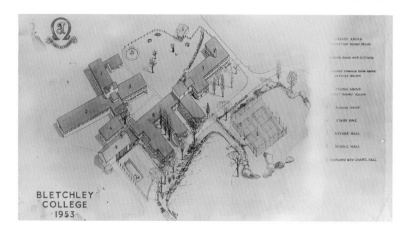

Bletchley Park in 1953

Colossus, the world's first electronic digital computer

Aerial view, 1966

Above: Bombe machine under construction

Right: Bletchley Park in 2003

Breaking Enigma

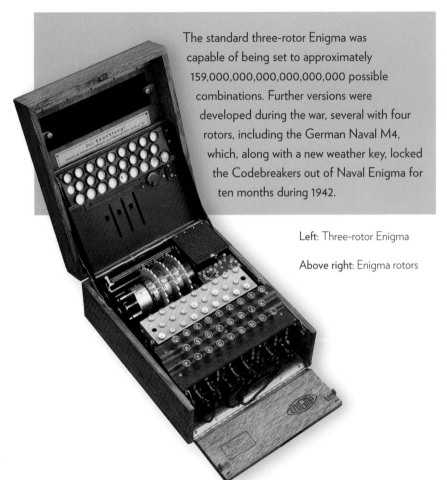

The standard three-rotor Enigma was capable of being set to approximately 159,000,000,000,000,000,000 possible combinations. Further versions were developed during the war, several with four rotors, including the German Naval M4, which, along with a new weather key, locked the Codebreakers out of Naval Enigma for ten months during 1942.

Left: Three-rotor Enigma

Above right: Enigma rotors

Above: Enigma rotors with numbered rings (German Army or Air Force)

The Enigma used rotors to scramble messages into unintelligible cipher text. The German military adapted an early commercial version, marketed to the banking industry, and believed it to be impenetrable. Each one of the machine's billions of possible combinations generated completely different cipher text. Finding those settings – most of which were reset at midnight every day – was the challenge faced by the Codebreakers.

Before World War Two, work was being undertaken in a number of countries to break Enigma. In July 1939, aware that Poland would soon be invaded, the Poles shared the work of their mathematicians who had worked on Enigma with the British and the French. By this time the Germans were changing most of the Enigma settings daily and the first British wartime breaks into the daily-changing Enigma code took place at Bletchley Park in January 1940.

The number of different possible settings for the Enigma machine are staggering. Each rotor could be set to any one of 26 different ring settings. Then the plug board could be set in a vast number of different ways. The settings were also different for the Army, Air Force, Navy and Secret Service, and most were changed daily. The main task of the Codebreakers was to deduce the daily Enigma settings, so the Bombe machine became vital.

Above: Bombe Room chart

Top left: Bombe drum

Top right: Rows of drums on the Bombe

The Bombe machine was developed by Alan Turing and Gordon Welchman to speed up the breaking of Enigma, so that messages were still operationally relevant. It was inspired by the 'Bomba', an earlier machine designed by the Polish Cypher Bureau. The Bombe helped to deduce the day's Enigma settings, of both the rotors and the plug board, by eliminating the many incorrect possibilities.

The Codebreakers created a menu for the wiring at the back of the Bombe based on a hypothesis, known as a 'crib', of part of the original message. Cribs were often derived from regular appearances in deciphered messages of stock phrases, such as 'message number' or 'nothing significant to report'.

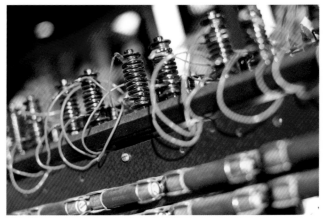

Above: Bombe wiring

Left: Enigma machine in use in General Heinz Guderian's command vehicle in France, May 1940

The drums on the Bombe each represented a rotor on the Enigma. The Bombe had 108 drums, each vertical set of three representing an Enigma machine. The drums were set to offsets corresponding to the menu being run and were connected with plug leads, again according to the menu, on the back of the Bombe. The drums were driven through all 17,576 positions, which took around 12 minutes.

If at one or more of the 17,576 positions the Bombe detected that the logic of the menu was satisfied, it would slow down and stop, supplying the Codebreakers with possible settings of the Enigma machine. The Codebreakers would check those settings on a checking machine and, utilising the intercepted message header, deduce the Enigma settings of the day. They would then apply those settings to a modified Typex machine – the British equivalent to Enigma – and type the enciphered message. If they'd got it right, plain German text came out, in groups of five letters. All of that day's intercepted messages on that network could then be deciphered using the Typex, and the Bombe could start on the settings of another network.

The Bombe sped up the process but a great deal of deduction was required both before and after the machine was run. Breaking into the new Enigma settings was a huge intellectual feat, which the Codebreakers achieved most days, usually in the middle of the night.

Right: Part of the keyboard of a teleprinter

Below: British cipher machine, Typex

Breaking Lorenz

Even more complex than the Enigma was the Lorenz cipher machine. It was used by Hitler himself, the High Command and German Army Field Marshals. It was much bigger and heavier than the Enigma and had twelve wheels. The Codebreakers called the machine Tunny and the coded messages Fish. Cracking Lorenz, like Enigma, relied on determining the starting position of the wheels.

Lorenz used the international teleprinter code, in which each letter of the alphabet was represented by a series of five electrical impulses. Extra letters were generated by the wheels and added to the original text. Five of the twelve wheels followed a regular movement pattern

Above: Inside the Lorenz attachment

Left: Lorenz cipher attachment

and two wheels dictated the movement pattern of the other five. To decrypt a message, the receiving Lorenz added the same obscuring letters.

The enciphered message was fed directly into a radio transmitter, which transmitted it to a distant receiving station. Here it was fed straight into a Lorenz machine. Both machines had to be set exactly the same way.

The Germans began using the Lorenz machine in the second half of 1940. The teleprinter signals were intercepted but the Codebreakers knew nothing about the machine being used to encrypt them. Then one German operator made a horrendous mistake.

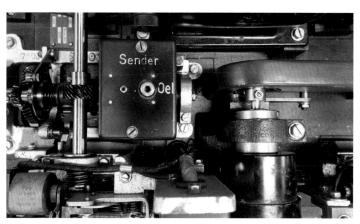

The mechanism of a Lorenz attachment

In August 1941 a long message was sent between Athens and Vienna. The operator transmitted a clear twelve-letter indicator which told the receiving operator the exact wheel start positions. He entered all 4,000 characters only to be told by the receiving operator that he hadn't got it. Assuming the system was unbreakable, the operator used the same settings and, because it was standard procedure, sent the indicator again. This time he abbreviated a number of words to save time.

The combination of the use of the same indicator and the abbreviations gave Bletchley's chief cryptanalyst John Tiltman a way in. It took Tiltman ten days but he recovered both German messages in full, thanks to the operator's mistake.

Bill Tutte, a Cambridge chemistry graduate, deduced through mathematical analysis how the Lorenz machine worked without ever

having seen one. A new section was set up to capitalise on Tiltman's and Tutte's achievements, called The Testery after its leader Ralph Tester, a former accountant who had lived and worked in Germany.

From mid-1942, intercepted Lorenz messages were punched into perforated teleprinter tape and sent via both teleprinter and dispatch rider to The Testery. There they were deciphered from gibberish to German.

By 1943 the Germans had introduced complications which made it virtually impossible to break Lorenz by hand – or brain – alone. The first machine designed by Dr Max Newman and his team in The Newmanry was christened Heath Robinson, after the cartoon designer of fantastic contraptions. It worked, but was slow and unreliable, so Max Newman called upon Tommy Flowers, a brilliant Post Office electronics engineer. Flowers designed Colossus, the world's first

Left: Colossus in operation, 1944

Above: Thyratron valves in a Colossus machine

Above right: Heath Robinson was slow and unreliable

Right: Colossus tape drive pulley

practical electronic digital and information processing machine – the forerunner of the modern computer. It would eventually use 2,500 thermionic valves (vacuum tubes) and the first Colossus machine arrived at Bletchley in January 1944.

Colossus could read paper tape at 5,000 characters per second, the paper tape in its wheels travelling at 30 miles per hour. This meant that the huge amount of mathematical work that needed to be done to break Lorenz could be carried out in hours, rather than weeks.

The first Colossus was joined by a second in June 1944, and was working in time for Eisenhower and Montgomery to be sure that Hitler had swallowed the deception plan prior to D-Day on 6 June 1944. There were eventually ten working Colossi at Bletchley Park.

Other Codes and Ciphers

Bletchley Park did not only break into Enigma and Lorenz. The Codebreakers also cracked a number of other ciphers being used by enemy forces during World War Two.

The Hagelin C38 for example, a Swedish machine, was introduced in 1938 and used by the Italian Navy, the US Navy and Army and the Royal Navy. The Italian system was broken by Bletchley Park, giving details of the convoys taking German troops and supplies to North Africa.

Above: Inside the Hagelin C38

Left: Hagelin C38 cipher machine

Significant effort went into breaking Japanese codes too. Around 55 different systems were used during the course of World War Two. Most were numeric but some lower-grade messages were encoded using letter-based ciphers. The sheer size of the Pacific helped the Allies, as it meant keys and codebooks were rarely replaced because it was impractical to send out new ones too often, over such great distances. So once the Allies broke into a code, they had a longer window than with other cipher systems before it was changed.

There were other cipher systems which didn't even involve machines. A book cipher codenamed Barbara is an example of paper-based systems. It was based on a double transposition cipher and was used by Germany to send weather reports. John Tiltman broke into this system in March 1940.

Left: The SG-41, intended to replace Enigma. It was never broken but production problems and the end of the war prevented it from being successfully deployed

Below: Relays in a Sturgeon machine

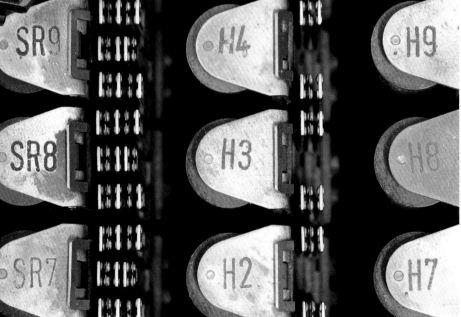

The Development of the Bletchley Park site

Bletchley Park is unique. It housed a collection of brilliant minds tasked with codebreaking during World War Two, thereby altering the course of history.

The surviving fabric of Bletchley Park shows every stage of the advances made in cryptographic, computing and intelligence processes. War work at Bletchley Park began in The Mansion, then expanded into hastily built timber huts and, later, brick, steel and concrete blocks, most of which still stand today.

The decision to give the codebreaking operation the resources it needed to expand was given urgency by Winston Churchill himself in 1941, when he encouraged his Chiefs of Staff to 'Action this Day' requests from Bletchley. This urgency reflected the pressures of total war. The construction of the blocks marked the Allies' transition from defensive to offensive military operations, including the bomber offensive, the break-out from North Africa and preparations for the invasion of Europe.

Above: Bletchley Park July 1940

Right: View from The Mansion in 1945

Above: View from Hut 2

Right: Map showing the development of Bletchley Park 1939-45, courtesy of English Heritage

The development of the huts and blocks, from the original nucleus centred on The Mansion and Stableyard, shows how codebreaking was industrialised and is a testament to the development of information technology. Bletchley Park is now a unique surviving example of a country house and park adapted for wartime use, and typifies developments at hundreds of country homes requisitioned for use during World War Two.

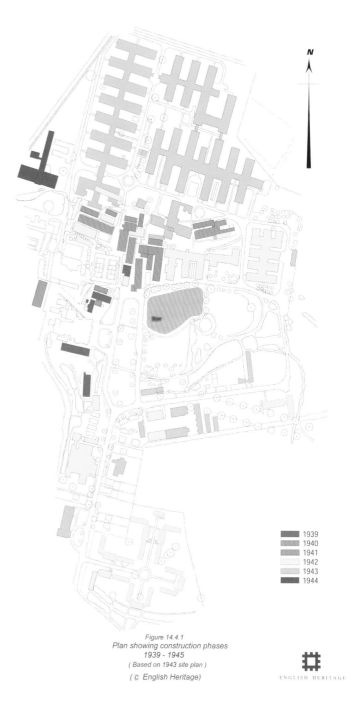

	1939
	1940
	1941
	1942
	1943
	1944

Figure 14.4.1
Plan showing construction phases
1939 - 1945
(Based on 1943 site plan)

(© English Heritage)

ENGLISH HERITAGE

The Mansion

The Mansion dates back to the late 1870s. It was bought in 1883 by Sir Herbert Leon, a wealthy stockbroker, along with the surrounding estate and was occupied by him, his wife Lady Fanny and family. He added an opulent new south front and lavish interior around 1906.

During World War Two, The Mansion served as the headquarters and recreational building. The major codebreaking sections initially worked on the ground floor, before the expansion into the huts. The main cafeteria was housed in the Dining Room until April 1942. The Mansion also housed the offices of senior staff such as John Tiltman, head of the Military Section, Commander Alastair Denniston, head of GC&CS from 1919 to February 1942, and Commander Edward Travis, head from 1942 and the first post-war head of GCHQ.

The Mansion – known by Bletchley Park workers, both military and civilian, as The Main House – was the iconic structure of the site. The area of the Park in front of The Mansion and Stableyard conveys the strongest sense of Bletchley Park's wartime atmosphere, and features strongly in published memoirs of wartime Bletchley.

The first telephone exchange was in the Billiard Room. Later a larger exchange was built in a blast-proof hut immediately behind Hut 4. The building which now houses the Enigma Cinema was later built to house the main switchboard for the many teleprinters, leaving the one behind Hut 4 for telephones.

Until the expansion which began in late 1941, everyone ate in the Dining Room, but once the canteen had been built the Dining Room

The Mansion before World War Two

The Leon family's staff

was reserved for senior staff only. The canteen still stands in Wilton Avenue, outside the original World War Two entrance.

Codebreaker Mavis Batey (née Lever) recalled it not being quite as egalitarian as intended, though:

'It all sounds very jolly … but none of the people I have spoken to remember it that way. I feel sure that the top brass didn't queue with us in the canteen but continued to use the Dining Room and other stately rooms for visiting VIPs.'

The parkland of Bletchley Park was used for playing games, drinking coffee in the open air – weather permitting – and as a place for non-smokers to clear their heads given the pipe-smoking culture which

Denniston made clear his intention to provide facilities for relaxation from the mental stresses of work. The first meeting of the Joint Committee of Control, which ran the internal organisation of Bletchley Park from 1941 to 1942, issued a memo which read:

'In my view we have reached a stage in the development of BP when our main and most serious drawback to efficiency and the sense of good feeling on which efficiency must depend, is not the absence of adequate space to work, but the absence of any place at all to play … somewhere where all can have their cup of coffee and cigarette without condemning the vast majority, seniors and juniors alike, to stand cheek by jowl like sardines in a tin.'

The peaceful Park

Lady Fanny Leon in The Morning Room

Left: The Mansion

Below: Griffins guard The Mansion entrance

Left: The Morning Room, former office of Cdr Alastair Denniston, the first Head of the Government Code and Cypher School

prevailed in the huts. Entertainment and consolation were sought by the Lake, which had been built more than two centuries earlier from the remains of medieval fishponds. Many romances also blossomed here.

The Mansion is open to visitors and contains information about its pre-war history.

Left: The Library, dressed as it looked during World War Two

Right: The Billiard Room

Stableyard

During World War Two there were three cottages on the north side of the Stableyard, the Apple and Pear Store on the south side, which later became known as the Bungalow, and the West Range, used for vehicles and carrier pigeons which received messages from occupied Europe.

Codebreakers, including Alan Turing and Dilly Knox, worked in the Cottages from September 1939. The first breaks into daily-changing German Enigma were made here. This success was kept secret even within Bletchley Park. The breaking of the German Secret Service (Abwehr) codes by Dilly Knox and his team, Illicit Signals Knox (ISK), in December 1941 supported the Double Cross operation prior to D-Day.

- The break into Italian Enigma that underpinned victory in the naval Battle of Matapan, off Crete in March 1941, was achieved in the Cottages
- Alan Turing and Gordon Welchman developed the first electromechanical Bombe in the Bungalow

Codenamed Operation Fortitude South, the Double Cross operation led the Germans to believe that the Allied plan to invade Normandy was actually a diversion from the true target, the Pas de Calais. This allowed the Allies to land at Normandy while the Germans laid in

The Garages in wartime

The Garages today

fortified wait in Calais. Abwehr Enigma messages broken in the Cottage made it clear that Germany had swallowed the deception whole.

The Cottages were also home to the Head of Works Services, Mr Budd and his family – including twin daughters who were six years old when they arrived at Bletchley Park. The Budds were one of only two families who lived on site.

Today in the Stableyard the Polish Memorial commemorates the achievements of the three mathematicians – Marian Rejewski, Henryk Zygalski and Jerzy Różycki – who broke Enigma using mathematical methods in 1933 and handed their work on Enigma to the British in 1939, helping to advance the codebreaking efforts of the Allies.

The Cottages

Beyond the garages is the gate where most of the dispatch riders arrived. As many as forty riders delivered up to 3,000 messages a day.

The Stableyard now houses the offices of the Bletchley Park Trust.

The Clock Tower in wartime

The Clock Tower undergoing repair

The Polish Memorial

Hut 6

Hut 6 was built in January 1940 for the decryption of Enigma messages from the German Army and Air Force. Initially the work was conducted with help from perforated sheets which were known as Zygalski sheets after the Polish Codebreaker who invented them. The Bletchley Park Codebreakers referred to these as Netz and they were used to help deduce part of each Enigma key. Later efforts were assisted by the Bombe machines initially located in Huts 11 and 11A.

Once the day's Enigma settings had been partially established with help from the Bombes, the information was sent back to Hut 6 where it was used to complete the discovery of the Enigma settings. Decrypted messages were then passed to Hut 3 for translation and analysis.

A specially built chute was created to send decrypts securely to Hut 3. It was not as high-tech as many of Bletchley Park's wartime innovations; a broom handle was used to convey a wire basket containing messages between the two huts. There were complaints about the draught coming in from the chute and a carpenter was called in to install flaps at either end. This put an end to the method of alerting the other hut that a message was coming – calling out – and the sender moved on to banging the chute with the broom handle instead.

Hut 6 has been restored to its wartime condition and is open to visitors.

Above right: Hut 6 Control Room in Block D

Right: Machine Room, Hut 6 in Block D

Above: Inside Hut 6

Above right: Inside Hut 6

Right: Hut 6, wartime scene of Army and Air Force codebreaking

Hut 3

Once German Army and Air Force Enigma messages had been decrypted in Hut 6, they were passed next door to Hut 3 for translation and analysis. It was also the main reporting centre for enciphered teleprinter messages, named Fish by the Codebreakers, decrypted in The Testery and Newmanry in Block F.

The translators in Hut 3 had to make German military language, strictly formatted and littered with jargon, read like a credible report from a fake spy. Most recipients were never told that a message had come from Bletchley Park, nor that it was based on intercept.

The writer and poet F.L. Lucas, who worked in Hut 3, said 'It was not a matter of receiving straightforward messages and translating them: it was always a matter of receiving material which was nearly always more or less imperfect, often incomplete, rarely intelligible with ease, and at its worst totally meaningless to even the best German scholar.'

Hut 3 pre-restoration

Newly restored Hut 3 with authentically dressed rooms

As the importance of the work carried out in the huts grew, so did the number of staff needed. By 1942 Hut 3 activity was no longer housed in a single wooden structure but in a whole range of locations and buildings around Bletchley Park. This is also true of the other huts.

Hut 3 has been restored to its wartime condition and is open to visitors.

Chris Hayes, one of the young women recruited to work at Bletchley Park, recalled 'I was told to report to Bletchley railway station, and walk up to The Main House for an interview. I was not told the nature of the work before I got there, and have kept quiet about it for the past fifty years! I was sent to Hut 3, and my younger sister Lola Horan joined me at Bletchley Park six months later and was sent to Hut 6.'

Hut 3 pre-restoration

The newly restored Hut 3

Hut 8

Hut 8 was built in January 1940 for the decryption of raw material from the Navy. The first break into naval Enigma – codenamed Dolphin – early in 1941 had a significant impact on the Battle of the Atlantic. Information decrypted in Hut 8 helped to reduce the destruction wrought by the U-Boats in the Atlantic.

Under its heads Alan Turing and then Hugh Alexander Hut 8, like Hut 6, also became a major driving force in the development of analytical machines to speed up the decryption process.

Even after the naval Enigma operation moved to Block D it was still called Hut 8. The old hut was renamed Hut 18. During the D-Day landings intercept operators were based there to ensure swift warning of any German naval attacks.

Hut 8 today

Naval Enigma was broken in Hut 8

Hut 8 at the end of the war

Alan Turing used his office in Hut 8 to write academic papers in his spare time, some of which are now on show in the Block B Turing Exhibition.

In Hut 8 visitors can see Alan Turing's office and test their codebreaking skills in the Brilliant Minds Exhibition

Above: Departments retained their hut names when they later moved into blocks

Right: Alan Turing chained his mug to the radiator to prevent it being stolen

Hut 4

Before the arrival of GC&CS, the Library in The Mansion looked out over a beautiful rose garden.

Originally housing the German Air Force and Naval Sections, from mid-1940 the main function of this hut was translating and analysing German naval Enigma messages decrypted by Hut 8. These two huts provided crucial day-to-day intelligence in the desperate battles between the Allied convoys and the U-Boats which were determined to cut Britain's vitally important supply lines across the Atlantic.

Hut 4 viewed through The Mansion windows

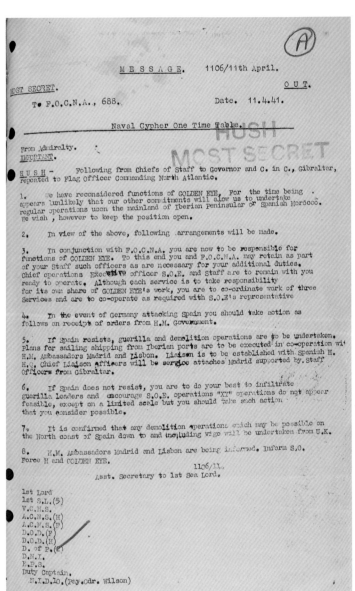

'Most Secret' later became 'Top Secret'

Early in the war, relations between the Naval Section in Hut 4 and the Admiralty were strained, as many in Naval Intelligence were unconvinced of the reliability of information emerging from Bletchley Park. But in 1941 the Enigma system being used by the U-Boats, codenamed Dolphin, was broken thanks to a combination of repetitive weather transmissions and a captured book of Enigma keys. This was a major breakthrough. Dolphin was broken and then read every day until the end of the war.

Today Hut 4 houses the café.

Above right: Children's Play Area outside Hut 4

Right: Hut 4 now houses the café

Huts 11 & 11A

Hut 11 was built to house the Bombe machines developed by Alan Turing and Gordon Welchman to speed up the daily search for the Enigma cipher keys used by the German Army, Air Force, Navy and Secret Service. It replaced a smaller, wooden hut, the concrete structure providing the protection needed for such precious machines.

Bombes were eventually mass-produced. Two buildings at Bletchley Park were given over to housing them initially, but there were far more at outstations in local villages and as far away as Eastcote and Stanmore on the outskirts of London. Even more were produced and operated in the United States. Hut 11A became the main control centre for all Bombes in the UK.

Hut 11A was built in March 1942, as more Bombes were needed and made, and it also became a training centre for the Women's Royal Naval Service – WRNS, known as 'Wrens' – who operated the machines and nicknamed this hot and noisy hut the 'Hell Hole'.

Wrens operated the Bombe machines

Hut 11

The first Newmanry was established here in 1943, under Max Newman. This section developed machines to help decipher German teleprinter codes. These two huts provided a highly secure environment for the crucial machines.

Hut 11 has recently been restored to its wartime layout and now tells the story of the people who worked there. Hut 11A will also soon be brought back to life and opened to the public.

A typical Bombe room with the WRNS operators

Inside Hut 11 today

Hut 1

Hut 1 was one of the first to be built. Its initial purpose was to house the MI6 wireless transmission station which was originally in The Mansion's water tower. Aerials were strung from The Mansion to the tall trees at the front.

The first Bombe machine, Victory, was tested in Hut 1 in early 1940, in what was then a sick bay. Later in the war Hut 1 became the Transport Office. A mere handful of the Codebreakers lived on site, the rest being billeted around Bletchley and the surrounding countryside and having to get to and from the site in large numbers for the three eight-hour shifts each day and night.

Hut 1 is open to the public.

Hut 1

Hut 1

Remnants of Hut 1 wartime bomb blast wall

Hut 12

Hut 12 started as an annex to Hut 3, and later became part of Hut 4's naval Enigma operation. It then housed the Intelligence Exchange, with cryptanalyst Nigel de Grey at the helm.

Ian Fleming, the James Bond creator, worked for Naval Intelligence and was responsible for liaising with Bletchley Park. He planned an operation to capture a naval Enigma machine, Operation Ruthless, which never came to fruition, but the qualities he described in the operative it would need were remarkably similar to the 007 character he later created.

By April 1943 Hut 12 was known as the Education Hut, used for chamber music classes and orchestral evenings held by the BP Musical Society.

Today Hut 12 is open to the public.

Above: Hut 12

Wartime BP Musical Society used Hut 12

A

CONCERT OF

ENGLISH MUSIC

BY THE

B.P. MUSICAL SOCIETY

(Conductor - HERBERT MURRILL)

IN THE

Assembly Hall, Wilton Avenue,

FRIDAY, SEPT. 8th,
SATURDAY, SEPT. 9th,
MONDAY, SEPT. 11th,
TUESDAY, SEPT. 12th,

at 8 p.m. sharp.

Programme : Sixpence.

All Proceeds to
The Sailors', Soldiers' and Airmens' Families Association.

Creativity thrived at Bletchley Park

Block A

In March 1941 a decision was made which would alter the landscape and layout of Bletchley Park forever. The codebreaking factory had outgrown The Mansion, Cottages and wooden huts, and a programme of building more permanent brick and concrete blocks was begun.

The first of these was Block A. There was still a significant threat of air attack so Blocks A and B, which were built at the same time, were bomb-proofed and shrouded by trees, more being planted to break up shadows thrown by the moon.

Blocks A and B were meant to house all three sections, Naval, Air and Army. Staff working on the translation and analysis of naval Enigma messages initially moved to Block A from Hut 4 in August 1942, but by mid-1943 the Naval section had taken over the building, such was the volume of messages it was decoding. Huge charts of the Atlantic covered the walls.

Today much of Block A is commercial offices.

Above: Steel, brick and concrete blocks were built from 1941

Left: Some blocks were reinforced against bomb blasts

Block E

Block E was the hub of outward communication from Bletchley Park. Messages were re-enciphered using Typex machines and transmitted to Allied headquarters.

Special Communication Units (SCUs) passed the highly sensitive Ultra intelligence to a Special Liaison Unit (SLU). An SLU officer would personally deliver the Ultra message to the Allied commander in the field, allow him to read and absorb, then destroy it.

No mention was made of Bletchley Park. Cover stories were used, such as 'a reliable source recovered a flimsy bit of a message in the wastepaper basket of ...'. To avoid enemy suspicion that Enigma was being read, information had always to be verified, and reconnaissance aircraft were sometimes sent, merely so they might be spotted by the enemy.

Block E is currently used as commercial office space.

Charts covered the walls for calculations and mapping

Block E was a communications hub

Secrecy was absolute

Typex machines were used to re-encrypt outgoing messages

Block B

Block B was built along with Block A, as Bletchley Park grew into a mechanised codebreaking factory. Block B was hardened, like Block A, in case of attack. In mid-September 1942 the remainder of the staff working on the translation and analysis of naval Enigma messages moved here from Hut 4.

The German Navy had introduced a fourth rotor to the Enigma machines being used by the U-Boats. This vastly increased the number of possible settings. Shaun Wylie, head of the Hut 8 Crib Section, said, 'We knew it was coming. But it was a grim time. We realised that our work meant lives and it ceased to be fun.'

Today, Block B houses various exhibitions and galleries relating to wartime Bletchley Park.

Block B and the Public Memorial to the Veterans of Bletchley Park and its Outstations

Buildings were stripped out and re-allocated as the operation expanded and was re-organised

The museum in Block B

Blocks F & H

During World War Two Block F became the world's first purpose-built computer centre. The Newmanry and The Testery moved in with Colossus, the world's first working electronic computer, invented by engineer Tommy Flowers to speed up the breaking of the fiendishly complex Lorenz cipher.

Block F also housed the Japanese codebreaking sections. It was demolished in 1988.

> The first Colossus arrived at Bletchley Park in 1944. By the end of the war there were ten. Donald Michie, a member of The Newmanry, said, 'Each one was like a very big wardrobe. It was a scene you didn't see again until about 1960 with huge main-frames, going flat out around the clock.'

Block H was built in 1944 and housed Colossus and Robinson machines.

Today Block H houses The National Museum of Computing.

Lorenz (aka Tunny) Room

The Testery was housed in Block F

Block C

Names of people, places, cover names, military units, radio stations and many other significant details were recorded and kept in an enormous index, punched onto cards using Hollerith machines. Clerks, mainly women, searched deciphered messages for details that might help the Codebreakers in the future, and built up a huge cross-referencing system. At its peak, two million cards per week were used.

This was originally housed in Hut 7 under the leadership of Frederick Freeborn, but in November 1942 it moved to the new, soundproofed, brick-built Block C. Different machines were used for punching the cards, sorting and collating, and they varied in size from similar to a typewriter up to a piano. Although it was a tried and tested technology, the machines were continually adapted in conditions of absolute secrecy.

Block C is now the Visitor Centre.

Card Index files in Block C

Block C

Machine Room, Block C

Block C now houses the Visitor Centre

The level of secrecy the Codebreakers worked under is sometimes difficult to imagine in the information age we live in today. Bletchley Park provided the Allies with an unprecedented wealth of intelligence on the enemy's movements and plans. This intelligence was given the codename ULTRA. Only a handful of top commanders were privileged to receive it, but were forbidden to act upon it until the Germans had been deceived into thinking the information could have come from another source. The need-to-know principle was paramount, even at Bletchley Park itself. Few staff knew the whole story or even which other sections existed besides their own, much less what they all did.

Inside the newly restored Block C before fit-out

Block D

Block D was built for secrecy, both inside and out. Its layout – with spurs off a corridor – was designed to keep different departments separate, so that staff knew only what they needed to. Around a thousand people worked here and a pneumatic tube system and conveyor belt were installed to speed up communication.

One spur housed the American contingent. The number of United States personnel connected to Bletchley Park eventually reached around 230. It was here that the 'special relationship', initiated politically by Winston Churchill and President Roosevelt, was firmly cemented into British-United States affairs.

When Block D opened, all the staff working in Huts 3, 6 and 8 moved in and it became the heart of Bletchley Park's operation to break Enigma messages. It also housed the Hut 6 traffic analysis section known as SIXTA, which helped build a picture of the German order of battle. Much intelligence planning and decoding for the Normandy invasion took place within these walls.

Above: Sovex convey system in Block D

Below: Block D remains derelict

One key figure in the D-Day deception, which led Hitler to believe the Normandy landings were a diversionary tactic to draw his troops away from the real target, the Pas de Calais, was a Spanish spy named Garbo. He was a double agent, who invented a network of no less than 27 fictitious spies, claiming expenses for them all from Germany. Bletchley Park was able to read messages sent between the German Secret Service (Abwehr) and Garbo's controller in Spain, which showed that the Abwehr fully believed the deception.

Block D also gives us an idea of how the now demolished Block F might have looked.

Block D is currently derelict, but the Bletchley Park Trust has long-term plans for its restoration.

The interior of Block D today

US serviceman working at Bletchley Park

An imposing entrance to Block D

People

During World War One Britain built up a significant Signals Intelligence operation, listening to enemy radio traffic. The Government Code & Cypher School (GC&CS) was created at the end of the war and developed over the next two decades. By 1939 veteran cryptanalysts from World War One such as John Tiltman, Dilly Knox, Hugh Foss and Frank Birch, plus linguists and classicists, formed the core of GC&CS's expertise. They were joined by men and women recruited from industry and other branches of academia. This eclectic mix of people, together with the rarefied atmosphere of Bletchley Park and the great sense of its work's importance, made for a unique experience.

The Bletchley Park Recreational Club included a library, drama group, music and choral societies as well as bridge, chess, fencing and Scottish dancing. Wrens drafted in to operate the Bombes were billeted together at local country houses including Woburn Abbey, and the 'Wrenneries' became renowned for their dances.

Rounders on the Lawn

Bletchley Park had a thriving amateur dramatics scene

Skating on the Lake, January 1940

Musical and theatrical productions were popular

Fencing at Bletchley Park

Many romances blossomed here, and numerous couples went on to marry. But they had all signed the Official Secrets Act and kept their vow of silence until the story of what was achieved here began to emerge in the 1970s. Then, and even now, some remain tight-lipped about their part in the codebreaking operation because they had sworn to do so.

Many of the Codebreakers went on to achieve high positions in academia, business and politics after the war. Some played a key role in developing GCHQ, as GC&CS was renamed.

Women outnumbered men at Bletchley Park by around three to one

Women made up the majority of the personnel at Bletchley Park, and not only in supporting roles: they made a significant contribution to the codebreaking. The working culture was described by American cryptographer William Friedman as one where 'Rank or status cuts no ice'.

Restoration

Bletchley Park is the historic home of the World War Two Codebreakers. The remarkable work that took place here made a profound and decisive difference to the outcome of the war. 2014 is a landmark year for Bletchley Park, following 22 years of hard work by the Bletchley Park Trust, and sees the completion of the first phase of essential restoration to the landscape, the Codebreaking Huts and the transformation of Block C into a Visitor Centre.

The next phase of the project to restore Bletchley Park is expected to cost in the order of £20 million and take ten years to complete. This will enable the Bletchley Park Trust to restore the remaining historic buildings, currently derelict or not fit for use, and to further develop its educational programme and exhibitions for ever-increasing numbers of visitors.

The Bletchley Park Trust has a responsibility to safeguard this important site for future generations, in permanent and fitting tribute to those extraordinary people who worked here during World War Two, and to tell their stories in the buildings in which they undertook the work that helped change the very course of history.

Block C during restoration

Block C during restoration

'The work here at Bletchley Park ... was utterly fundamental to the survival of Britain and to the triumph of the west. I'm not actually sure that I can think of very many other places where I could say something as unequivocal as that. This is sacred ground. If this isn't worth preserving, what is?'
Professor Richard Holmes, Military Historian

Block C exhibition fit-out

Restoration of iconic Codebreaking Huts

Returning the landscape to its wartime parkland

The Impact of Bletchley Park

Winston Churchill, the British Prime Minister, was an ardent supporter of Bletchley Park and had absolute belief in the intelligence generated by the Codebreakers, referring to them as 'the geese that laid the golden egg and never cackled'. When the top Codebreakers wrote to him in 1941, starved of resources to do their essential work, Churchill ordered 'Action this day! Make sure they have all they want on extreme priority and report to me that this has been done.'

'The intelligence ... from you [Bletchley Park] ... has been of priceless value. It has saved thousands of British and American lives and, in no small way, contributed to the speed with which the enemy was routed and eventually forced to surrender ... [It was a] very decisive contribution to the Allied war effort.'
General Dwight D. Eisenhower

'So, if I may say so, you (The Bletchley Park Trust) are the keepers of one of the greatest British success stories.'
HRH The Prince of Wales

Memorial designed by Charles Gurrey, unveiled by HM The Queen in July 2011

Granny Mary's Pies, Puddings and Passions

CW00358024

*A book of plain and simple recipes,
a few home-decoration ideas,
reflections on a life in and
around Hathersage,
– and many lovely
pictures to look at.*

Granny Mary's Pies, Puddings and Passions

Published in the UK by

Hucklow Publishing

Ash House, Great Hucklow, Derbyshire SK17 8RF

November 2011

© Mary Bailey 2011

ISBN: 978-0-9563473-4-3

All rights reserved. No part of this publication may be reproduced, stored in a retrieval system, or transmitted, in any form or by any means, electronic, mechanical, photocopying, recording or otherwise, without the prior permission of Hucklow Publishing.

This book is sold subject to the condition that it shall not, by way of trade or otherwise, be lent, re-sold, hired out or otherwise circulated without the prior consent of Hucklow Publishing in any form or binding or cover other than that in which it is published and without a similar condition including this condition being imposed on the subsequent purchaser.

Artwork and Layout Designed by Hucklow Publishing

Printed by Northend Creative Print Solutions
Sheffield

Food, fun, friendship and faith – what better ingredients for sustaining a good life. *(Rupert St John Brigham Wade)*

If you're sitting comfortably . . . .

Sitting snug and warm on the fender in front of my Yorkshire range on a very cold, snowy, December day, my thoughts drifted to the changing seasons and the inspiration came to me for a second book.

When Michael got home that night, having battled through all the ice and snow, I excitedly told him I'd had a good idea. When he realised that no supper was forthcoming because I'd been too busy thinking about my idea, he calmly walked into his office, switched on the computer and wrote 'Here we go again'. So volume two was born.

Michael was happy I'd started this project as it gave me real purpose; I'd not been feeling well for some time and it was just the therapy I needed. Friends started to say, "Mary's back", not knowing what secret mischief I was up to and oblivious to the tasting samples with which I innocently plied them.

The seeds for the new book were well and truly sown in my mind by the time my favourite season of Advent was upon us. 'Advent isn't a season', I hear you cry, but for me, it is the fifth season and the most important of all as it's the time of positivity and looking forward ; looking forward to what is entirely up to the individual, one's beliefs and expectations and what better starting point for this book.

This is not merely a recipe book or a book of recipes – it's also a bit of this, a bit of that, and a bit of the other. I wanted to share not only my recipes but things that have made me who I am – my great passion for the changing seasons, for animals and flowers, and some of the people, things and occasions that have been so influential in my life.

When I first got to work on the contents everything was pastry and pies, so when asked what I was up to my usual reply was 'Pies and Stuff', which became the original working title for the book. As work progressed other things crept in and we got way beyond just pies – so at the last minute I have been persuaded by my 'Literary Agent' to change the title to one which more fully expresses the content – so here goes with *Granny Mary's Pies, Puddings and Passions.*

For all my friends and family who over the last fifty years have enjoyed company and meals around this kitchen table.

Here's to meals and years to come, with my love.

Carr Head – much as I knew it in my growing up years.

My father and his parents outside Kimber Court

My Mum, Elsie

Me – flower arranging at an early age

Granny Mary and uncle Roly with some of their produce outside Cutter's Cottage on Church Bank, now home of one of my dearest friends, Liz T.

Growing Up

I grew up at a place called Kimber Court, with my father, Joe Thorpe, my mother, Elsie, my maternal granny, Mary Underwood, and my mother's brother, uncle Roly. This was my father's family farmhouse situated at the top of a narrow winding lane on the hillside above Hathersage village. The next house below us was Moorseats, a large rambling place occupied by three spinster sisters, the Misses Hodgkinson – Vera, Enid and Monica. Down the lane beyond Moorseats was Carr Head, home of the Barber family, Jarvis, Mo and Andy.

My mother died when I was only six and a half. I was at Carr Head with Mo and Andy when she died, and Mo took me under her wing, became my second mother and saw me through my early growing up years; she herself died only recently.

Electricity didn't arrive in our little part of the world until the early 50s so there was no fridge or freezer, and food was kept in the larder. I remember going into the larder where a long steel rail with hooks went across the space near the window, and this is where, aged 3, I learnt to count . . . the tails of the fluffy bunnies! My best number was 26, and I thought I was very clever. My uncle Roly had 'taken care of' them from the rabbit population on the hillside. Many a family was very grateful for a gift of a rabbit from him.

Mo once said she didn't know what they would have eaten between 1940 and 1945 if it wasn't for Asa the village butcher and my Granny Underwood. She artisanally fashioned every part of the pig into wonderful tasty food for Carr Head, Moorseats and Kimber. It was presented on a very large wooden tray. Mo said, on its arrival, she often cried with grateful thanks.

I have fond memories of my childhood, mostly spent wandering between Carr Head, visiting Mo and Andy, and Moorseats to see 'Misty' the old smelly sheepdog whom I adored. Apparently I was known to have an afternoon nap in her basket with her under what was know as the 'Maid's stairs'.

As a child, I was totally unaware that food was on ration and meat was scarce - we were just lucky and very popular. My granny was very kind and generous to friends who had a need and nobody ever visited and went home empty-handed. Granny's freshly made butter would be on a slab in the pantry, all marked out in a pattern with an imprint on top. I loved to go in and put my fingers in and taste it; that lovely salty, creamy taste, never to be forgotten. She could have made a churn full on a Friday to last the week but by Sunday evening, after a weekend of visitors, there would be nothing left. The same with eggs, jams, black puddings, haslet, savoury ducks, brawn, potted meat, bread and teacakes. I have never tasted teacakes like them with all that beautiful butter on. However, she did complain about never having enough yeast or sugar but I think she had an arrangement with the local shop and a bit of bartering must have taken place!

My love of cooking and kitchen things stems from that time, and much of what appears in this book was inspired by it.

Some ingredients in the recipes might sound extravagant but you have to remember that we were farmers; things like meat, game, poultry, butter, milk, mushrooms, cream, eggs, walnuts, hazelnuts, horseradish, vegetables, potatoes, soft fruit, were all on the farm or hillside, growing wild just like me! And that hillside, where I still live, holds the deep roots of my history, my traditions, and my way of life.

Measures and Conversion Tables

Weight

Ounces	Grams
1/2	15
1	30
2	55
3	85
4	115
5	140
6	170
7	200
8	225
9	255
10	285
11	310
12	340
16	455

Temperature

Centigrade C	Farenheit F	Gas
110	225	slow
120	250	slow
130	265	1
140	280	1
150	300	2
160	310	3
170	325	3
175	350	4
180	360	5
200	400	6
210	410	7

Liquid

Pints	ml
1/4	142
1/2	284
1	568
2	1136

Fl oz	ml
4	114
8	227
16	454
32	909

A 'communion' of wine – as big as you can gulp.

Please Note – I still deal in Imperial measures, so my conversions to Metric are a little fluid. It's only a guide.

Index of Recipes

Soup Stuff

Always best to begin with a 'starter' –

Many people baulk at making soup.

Some say it's so expensive, others say it takes so much time and makes their kitchen smell. I say, so what? Yes, kitchens should be well ordered and good to look at but they are essentially working areas – that's what kitchens are for. And it's worth the occasional lingering cooking odour just for the pleasure the results can give to your friends and family.

Remember, if you can cope with making a larger amount in a single soup-making session then it freezes well, so you always have a meal at your finger tips – especially for those unexpected visitors.

Bonus: *making a large amount for freezing means the kitchen smells of it only once.*

NOTE

Allergies and Food Intolerances

I have friends with a variety of food intolerances so do please be mindful of this when cooking for family and friends; it's always best to ask first rather than upset them. Consider these common food allergies: wheat, shellfish, peppers, onions, **GARLIC**, dairy, peanuts, nuts in general; and I'm sure you'll know many more.

Chowder

Ingredients

1lb (455g)	either smoked haddock or cod, or mixed fish
2 pints (1.2 litres)	fish stock or water
1	bay leaf
2	sweet onions - peeled and sliced
8oz (225g)	potatoes - peeled and diced
1	stick of celery - chopped finely
2oz (55gm)	English butter
2 tbs	flour
½ pint (275ml)	fresh cream
3 rashers	smoked streaky bacon - cut into matchstick pieces.

Method

- Using a sauté pan, simmer the fish in the water or stock for 10 minutes. Drain off the liquid and **SAVE**.
- Discard the skin and bones and then flake the fish and keep on one side.
- Using the same pan, sweat the bacon slowly over a low heat until it sizzles and turns a golden brown. Add the butter, onions, celery, and potatoes and fry for a further 5 minutes.
- Draw the pan to the side and stir in the flour. Gradually add the strained fish juices and season lightly. Return to the heat for approximately 15 minutes until the potatoes are tender. If you feel it requires more liquid add milk to make the right consistency. If it is too thick it may burn the bottom of the pan. **Beware** - keep stirring, do not boil.
- Spoon in cream and fish, check seasoning and heat to the serving temperature. Garnish with lots of parsley or store until required.

This is a really hearty main course soup – delicious.

Variations:

As a variation you may like to 'push the boat out' and add shrimps, prawns, or mussels

Roasted Butternut Squash Soup

Ingredients

2 pts (1.2 litres) stock good chicken or vegetable

1 pt (568 mls)   milk

2   butternut squash - peeled, de-seeded and chopped into chunks

4   onions - peeled and sliced

6   carrots - peeled and chopped

4   parsnips - peeled and chopped

2oz (55g)   butter

3 tbs   olive oil

salt and pepper   to taste

Method

- To roast the butternut squash place the chunks in a roasting tin with a little olive oil. Cook in moderate oven for approximately 40 minutes.

- Fry the onions in half the butter and oil until golden; then put to one side.

- Likewise, fry the carrots and parsnips using the remaining oil and butter.

- Put the onions, carrots and parsnips into a large pan with enough stock. Gently bring to the boil then simmer for 10 minutes. Add a little more stock if needed.

- Add the butternut squash with 1 pint (570mls) milk to the pan and season with salt and pepper, simmer for a further 10 – 15 minutes.

- The soup must now be processed in a blender to a thick purée. Because of the volume you may have to deal with it in 3 or 4 lots. Whizz it until smooth. NB: **It's a heck of a colour**, so if you don't want it to re-decorate your kitchen make sure the top is on the blender first!

This quantity will feed 12 or so. If you do not need it all in one serving then make the full amount and freeze half the quantity – it freezes very well.

To serve you may need to dilute it a little more, and add a little more cream - go on. We love it really thick it's almost a meal in itself, delicious with home-made bread or cobs, whatever!

Creamy Mushroom Soup

Ingredients

1 lb (450g)	mushrooms - chopped (field mushrooms are best, if you can get them!)
2 large	onions - peeled and sliced
2 large tbs	flour - either plain or gluten free
½tsp	marmite
1 pint (570mls) stock	
2 – 3 knobs	butter
1 pint (570mls) milk	
1 tsp	mixed herbs - chopped finely
Small communion of sherry or Madeira (optional)	
salt and pepper	to taste

Method

- In a large pan melt half the butter and fry off the onions until a nice colour. Place in bowl with salt, pepper, herbs and flour mixed together.
- Next fry the mushrooms; they absorb butter very quickly so keep shuffling around or add more butter or oil.
- Put the onion mix back in with the mushrooms, add the milk, the stock and the marmite; gently bring up to the boil stirring continuously until the soup thickens, then turn down to simmer for approximately 15 minutes.
- If you wish to serve it straight away now is the time to put in the communion of sherry.
- If not, let it cool and store or freeze until required.

To Serve

Put into warm bowls with a swirl of cream on top. Decorate with a leaf or two of parsley and enjoy.

There is nothing to substitute the taste and flavour of freshly picked field mushrooms. We are lucky enough to be able to pick mushrooms in our own fields. Some weigh as much as 1lb or so. They come every year in exactly the same places. Isn't nature wonderful?

There is nothing quite like the taste of field mushrooms and we are so lucky to be able to pick them from our own fields.

My father's favourite meal was a couple of slices of bacon cut from the side hanging in the pantry fried with dripping in a pan on the Yorkshire range with some freshly made black pudding and field mushrooms. He would sit back to eat it while reading his Farmers Weekly, often with the cat fast asleep on or beside it – he called it "A meal fit for a King". On some days we had just bread and dripping.

In the 1940's our local butcher, Asa Littlewood, came up to the farm to kill the pigs. He sold the meat in his shop at the top of the village. He also had a slaughter-house in the middle of the village. It was much kinder in those days as the animals didn't have to be transported so far. Meat, of course, was on ration at this time. We put a side of bacon down by salting it on stone benches and hanging it on a hook in the pantry where it kept for quite a long time.

Thick Parsnip and Apple Soup

Ingredients

6 – 8	nice sized parsnips - peeled and chopped
3	onions - peeled and chopped
2 large	Bramley apples - peeled and sliced
2 pts (1.2 litres)	good stock - either vegetable or chicken
½ tsp	nutmeg
1	grated rind of an orange
	butter or corn oil
3 tbs	flour
	cream
salt and pepper to taste	

Method

- Take a large sauté pan.
- Soften the onions in the butter or oil for approximately 5 – 7 minutes.
- Do the same to the parsnips; then add the apple slices. After a few minutes pull off the heat.
- Put the flour in to thicken it, slowly pour in the stock, stir with a wooden spoon. Finally, add the nutmeg, orange rind, salt and pepper.
- Return to low heat and cook until tender - approximately 25 – 30 minutes. Stir from time to time.
- Liquidise until smooth.

When needed, reheat slowly then add cream, test the seasoning.

Serve with a swirl of cream and lots of parsley.

In my opinion this is a very comforting soup.

Special Red Pepper Soup

Ingredients

6 large	red peppers - peeled and de-seeded
Pkt	Rubiero pointed peppers - peeled and de-seeded
2 – 3	onions - peeled and chopped
2 – 3	sweet potatoes - peeled and cut into chunks
2 – 3	parsnips - peeled and cut into chunks
2 - 3 tbs	olive oil
2oz (55g)	butter
3½ - 4 pints	good stock (2.25 litres approx)
½ pt (284ml)	cream - to finish and serve
Salt and pepper	to taste

Method

- Place the peppers, potatoes and parsnips on two roasting tins, drizzle over with olive oil, sprinkle with salt and pepper, put towards the top of a moderate oven and roast for 40 minutes until tender.

- In a large sauté pan, melt the butter over moderate heat, add the onions and cook until coloured for about 5 minutes. Leave on the side with a lid on.

- Remove the roasted vegetables from the oven and put into the pan with the onions. Next put in stock and return to the heat bring up to simmering point. Let it simmer gently for 15 minutes or so. Add the cream at the end. Do not let it boil.

- Finally you must blitz it in the blender until smooth. Its best to do it in 3 or 4 goes. When you're ready to serve, taste it and add more seasoning if required. Also, if it's too thick for you, dilute with a little milk.

- Serve with a cream X (kiss) on the top and parsley. What a fabulous colour! This recipe makes a fair amount of good rich sweet soup. Good for freezing.

I first made this soup last year when the daughter went away leaving a fridge full of 'stuff' and rather than waste it I put It to good use. I've never seen so many peppers in a fridge in my life; four different kinds, there were some I'd never used before, so I thought here goes. Well this is the result and it's seriously good - believe me. The Bridge ladies loved it!

Cobs

I have always loved yeast baking, it is a pleasure to make and a pleasure to eat, however tiring it may have been. With the advent of the "Bread Maker" it has been made so much easier and one of the most useful features of the machine is the dough setting. This program usually takes about 1½ hours and will allow you to make a whole host of different breads. I have included two of them in this book.

The dough mixture

This is the same for both recipes

10 fluid ounces (300ml) warm milk

1 teaspoon salt

4 teaspoons sugar

1oz (30g) butter

16oz (500g) strong plain bread flour

1¼ teaspoons easy blend dried yeast

- Make the dough as per the instructions of your bread making machine. Some machines have a different cycle and the ingredients may need to be introduced in a different order.
- After the program has finished, take the dough out and put on a clean floured surface.
- Gently kneed the dough and cut into the required shapes and sizes; cover with clean tea-towel and leave to rise for 30 – 45 minutes.

- Pre-heat the oven to 200C (400F) and Gas 6 – remove the towel and brush tops with milk.
- Bake for 15 to 18 minutes until golden.
- Remove from oven and put on a cooling rack
- Rub tops with small amount of butter and a little sea salt

Onion, Olives and Tomato Bread

Method

Dough mixture as opposite.

Add a little fried onion, some chopped sun-ripe tomatoes and olives. Knead them into the mixture and shape into one flat cob.

Bake as opposite, but will take 20 to 25 minutes to cook.

Stuff and Nonsense

When granny died, I took charge of my uncle's house, aged just 13¾. I tried very hard to look after my younger sister, Margaret, my uncle and my father. It wasn't easy as I was still wrapped up in my own sadness, as were they in theirs. When someone so vital, the corner-stone of a family dies, it leaves a very big void.

The only grown-up friend I could turn to was Mrs Elsie Prince - one of my mother's and granny's friends - she understood my despair and was my salvation, and as a true Christian she guided me through my most troubled times. In the 1950's no-one gave, or expected 'outside' help or interference; you just got on with your 'lot'. My uncle told me that I had my responsibilities and I had to get on with them as best as I could.

My friends, Ann, Ray, Sue and I spent most of our summers at Hathersage swimming pool (which has just celebrated its 75th anniversary). They were happy days. After a cold swim we would warm up with a nourishing drink of Bovril. One day we walked into the café to find that a jukebox had been installed. At the age of fourteen I was ready to let my hair down a bit and the jukebox was a godsend - we had moved into the Rock n' Roll era! My first heart-stopper was Buddy Holly singing 'Peggy Sue' but that was nothing compared to what I felt when I heard Elvis for the first time.

Our only other entertainment in the village was the 'cinema' in the Memorial Hall. The pictures we saw wooed Sue to the USA and she has lived there now for almost fifty years. We four gals are still very close and she gets over to see us from time to time.

At this time I desperately wanted to go to Art School but my uncle would not allow it as he feared that I would turn into a 'beatnik'. Instead I went to work for Miss Hudson at the 'Corner Cupboard' (now 'Cintra's') where I made a lifelong friend of Margie, Miss Hudson's niece and Davy her nephew, who are the great great great grandchildren of the lady who is credited with devising the original Bakwell Pudding.

Margie went to Art School and worked at the café with me

Pretending to be a 'fast lady' – in Humphrey Davy Hudson's car outside Asa Littlewoods slaughter-house in the village.

in the holidays, as did her brother who was a terrible tease. His career was in the Army. It's still great fun when the Hudson family visit and we spend time reminiscing. I was reminded last year while talking to Margie how she and I always did an afternoon 'meander'; she loved to explore the churchyard examining the headstones.

On one particular windy day in September, we walked up to Carr Head to let Scramble the dog out. We opened the front door and the middle room door banged shut so violently that it brought the ceiling down! I said more than "Oh dear" but we couldn't stop laughing! Andy and I were to be married that October so it became just another room to decorate – it's just as well that I love decorating. Yes, I married the boy next door and since then Carr Head has been constant work and I still feel that I am a mere custodian. I was not twenty when I came here and I'm still decorating and stopping draughts.

In later years my children, Peter and Kim, were encouraged to have hobbies and pastimes, because I knew what trouble I was capable of getting into when I was their age if not kept occupied. Peter played (and was good at) cricket and later rode a trials bike like the rest of the family, something that remained a passion for him until this day. Kim was bequeathed a Donkey called Neddy who was lovely and gentle; the word got around and soon we had two more . . . Lucy and Moses. Later she progressed to ponies, and I still have visions of her flying around the back fields jumping over stone walls in a tweed flat cap with her long hair flailing behind her.

They were always arguing about stable space, Peter for his bikes and Kim for her four legged friends. I kept out of it and let them sort it out for themselves. I was always regarded by my friends as having a "laissez-faire" attitude which extended to turning a blind eye whenever either of them had a "party" at Carr Head. Thirty years on my grandchildren say to me about their mother (my daughter) "What she doesn't know won't hurt her" . . . maybe it's in the genes.

On bad weather days, when the Aga was on it's last legs, both the kids really enjoyed baking. They loved entering the cooking competitions in the Horticultural show and often did well. When I'm cooking with Charlie now, I often by mistake call him Peter, and he gives me "the look" as much to say, 'Granny . . . you're getting old!'

In 1977, the trusty old Aga finally died. I could not afford a new barrel for it so I decided it had to be taken out and disposed of, and for ease we decided to bury it in the garden. Our dear friend Ted volunteered for the task and it had to be removed in sections as it wouldn't go through the door. Our neighbour, Gordon, dug a deep hole with his JCB in the vegetable garden where it rested peacefully for several years until we had a really bad storm. The garden flooded and the two lids appeared which was a funny sight. By now, Michael was at Carrhead and was slowly learning about me and my eccentricities. He graciously covered up the lids and I planted some snowdrops to mark the spot.

In 2009 Charlie got a metal detector and tried it out in the garden. He came running in saying "Granny – Granny, I have found something really big." When I told him it was Aggie, he was at first a bit perplexed as he knew it could not be animal - it had to be mineral.

After the sad demise of Aggie, I had hoped we would have found the original range. When Mo put the Aga in around 1938/39, she said she remembered a range being behind it but sadly, some parts were there but not complete. In 1984 Michael and I were fortunate enough to find a replacement Yorkshire range. It's beautiful, made about 1880 by William Green and Co West Bar Sheffield, and it cost us all of £75. We installed it together over a Christmas period. I know how all the flues work, it gets hot enough to bake bread, heats the water, and provides a cosy kitchen on cold winter nights. As a family we all tend to congregate in the kitchen and invariably end up setting in a row on the fender in front of the Yorkshire range.

Peter and Kim
– the early years

Saddle of Lamb

Basic Stuff 1 – Stocks

Good stocks are a very important basic ingredient for so many dishes.

Beef Stock

Bones are the principal ingredient for beef stock, and the best bones are always from your local butcher, if you can get them, otherwise use stewing steak – this will cost more but it's worth it.

- Bones (or stewing steak), onions, carrots, leeks, celery, turnips, parsnips, or whatever is available. A few herbs, and salt and pepper.
- Put all the ingredients in a large pan and cover with water. Bring very slowly to the boil, put on lid, and simmer for 2 hours.
- Allow the liquid to cool, then take off the fat and remove the bones and the vegetables. Use as required, but it will keep in the fridge for several days. It is also good to freeze in portions, which means you will always have some to hand when necessary.

Chicken Stock

Make as above using a cooked chicken carcass. Perhaps this is the most useful stock. I sometimes buy a chicken just to make it into stock for the freezer.

Fish Stock

Again, follow the basic recipe above but this time using fresh fish complete with skin and bones, poached in milk and water.

Vegetable Stock

I make my stock when I'm either preparing vegetables, or after cooking them I save the liquid. Use the discarded tops of carrots, onions, leeks, celery etc and make sure they are clean then boil them up and strain, there you have it; season well. Keeps several days in the fridge.

Pork Stock

Specially for the pork pie.

Pigs trotters, a couple of onions, two pints of water, grated nutmeg, teaspoon of all-spice, salt and pepper, and sprigs of thyme, parsley and sage.

Put all ingredients into stock pot, as below, bring slowly to the boil, put on the lid and simmer for two hours. Allow liquid to cool before straining. Use as required.

The Preamble to the Pork Pie

To make a good pork pie there is one absolutely essential thing to remember: having assembled all the ingredients and before you start the process, **make sure you are not going to be disturbed**. Let the cat have your favourite chair and give the dog a bone. Do not answer the phone, do not be tempted to Text, Twitter, do Facebook or email – is that clearly understood? The making of a pork pie is more important and will require your full attention. Phone and text the world afterwards and tell them how clever you are.

Now the main reason I think that nobody seems to make pork pies these days is because people are afraid of making hot water-crust raised pastry. Well, I was nervous at first, but I've learnt a bit over the years, and I say don't be afraid, be confident and try it my way.

You will need to buy what is called a traditional pork pie tin ,or just use a very small loose-bottomed cake tin with high sides, and grease it well. Forget about stories you've heard about hand-raising the pastry round a glass jar, just mould it up the inside of your tin; it is a lot easier.

I have a view about the 'setting jelly', which not everybody likes. The way I recommend is to put jellied stock into the made filling, and when it's cold it sets. I've had no complaints so far, and I made over 100 testers for my friends in the village. The only complaint I've had from my testers and tasters is that I don't put in enough salt and pepper; well that's me and my taste – what you put in is up to you and your taste.

A good time of the year to practise making pork pies is in November, especially on a really cold winter's day when there is nothing else to do. I make them in several different sizes, but do think about the bigger versions for the Christmas season and New Year; make them as festive presents for family and friends, or take them to work instead of the 'mince pies', though that may be a step too far for some people.

I find it most difficult making small quantities of anything, and I would never consider putting the oven on just for one pie – it would have to be at least four. And I always make an extra one because we like to eat it straight away, hot from the oven. If you have never had home made hot pork pie - you don't know what you are missing. I do assure you once you've cracked it you will look at the pork pies bought in the shops quiet differently.

And trust me – they really do make a wonderful Christmas present.

How fortunate that here in Hathersage we have David Mellor's award winning cutlery factory, along with their best of kitchen shops, cafe, and small museum. Many of my large collection of kitchen utensils were bought there, purely and simply because they are of excellent quality, particularly their cake tins, and which double up wonderfully as great pork pie tins – they don't leak!

Pork Pie

Ingredients

Hot Water Pastry

1lb (455g)   plain flour

7oz (200g)   shortening i.e. butter, Cookeen or lard

7½ fl oz (210mls)   water/milk (equal parts)

1 tsp   salt, with pepper to taste

1 tsp   icing sugar

You will require a six-inch cake tin, or two small pork pie tins.

Filling – good quality filling is absolutely essential

6oz (170g)   diced pork

6oz (170g)   minced pork

2 rashes   chopped streaky bacon

3 large tbs of the pork pie stock

1 tbs   finely chopped herbs, ie sage, thyme and parsley

Bind all the ingredients together with the stock in a basin until required

Glaze   Egg and a little milk

Method – preheat the oven to 210C (410F, Gas 7)

To make pastry:

- For this pastry, instead of keeping everything cool - you keep everything warm. I suggest you put your bowl on the top of a wheat bag (the sort you take to bed for comfort) that has been in the microwave for 3 minutes. Place the wheat bag on the worktop, put the flour, icing sugar and seasoning in the bowl and cover with a tea towel.
- In a saucepan, put the milk, the water, and the shortening, and bring it just to the boil.
- Now the tricky part - pour the liquid into the flour and bring together with a wooden spoon. It is important that you work quickly, and I tend to use my hands. Continue until it comes together to form a pliable soft ball of dough (not too sticky). Gently knead together until it's smooth and elastic. It is similar to making bread.
- Take 2/3 of the dough, place in the bottom of the tin and start to work up the sides equally. Make sure the bottom is covered. You are now ready for the filling; press it down very gently, then egg wash the rim well.
- Make the top for your pie with the last bit of pastry; you may not need all of it, just as long as it has a nice even topping. Perhaps you would be happier to pat this down on a well floured work surface, or roll with a rolling pin.
- Lift the lid carefully and lower it down on top of the filling and press down well to seal the edges, make a pattern with your fingers around the top and make a small hole in the centre; egg wash well.
- Put on a baking tray (because sometimes it drips) place in the middle of the oven and bake at 210C (410F, Gas 7) for the first 20 minutes, turn down to 175C (350F, Gas 4) for 40 minutes or so, take a look. If you have a meat thermometer you can do a test: it has to be 77C (170F). I think it will need about 15 – 20 minutes more – different ovens may vary.

Gluten-free Pork Pie

I dedicate this pork pie recipe to Evie who had never tasted pork pie before. When she said she loved it I was thrilled. Quite a few of my friends are coeliac, meaning they cannot tolerate wheat.

Gluten-free flour is widely available now; the first time I used it to make a vegetable flan it was fairly successful. I then had a trial run at the 'Pork Pie'; well this wasn't as good – but now I've got the hang of it, I'm ready to pass this on, but there is a warning. Do not use commercially prepared sausages or sausage meat because they contain cereal - only use good quality pork from the butcher. If you tell them what you are making, they will prepare it for you. My local butchers "the Bowyer boys" are wonderful. If you tell them you're making Granny Mary's pork pie they sort you out with the right stuff.

For a 1lb pork pie follow this recipe, as previously using the one 6" deep cake tin or two small pork pie tins.

Method

Follow recipe for previous Pork Pie.

Be warned – the pastry doesn't behave like wheat flour and it feels more like cornflour; you'll find it makes your hands feel lovely.

Evie's picture of Granny Mary delivering the pork pie

Preserved Stuff

Chutney – All Seasons

Ingredients

4lbs (2Kg)	apples – peeled, cored and sliced
4lbs (2Kg)	other fruits, plums, cranberries, apricots, whatever (fresh or dried)
1lb (455g)	dates, chopped (stones removed)
1 lb	raisins
4 large	red onions - peeled and sliced
2 pts (1.2 litres) white pickling vinegar with spices (Sarson's is best)	
1oz (30g)	salt
	a little pepper
1lb (455g)	brown sugar

Method

- You will require a large preserving pan, or borrow one.
- Put all the ingredients into the pan, Add vinegar, salt and pepper and lastly brown sugar. Put on top of stove and stir frequently until boiling.
- Then turn down to simmer, stirring from time to time until thick and pulpy, it takes about 1½ to 2 hours. Check just like you would when making jam.
- While you are waiting for 'the set', sterilize your jars, you will need approximately 12 (screw-top are best).
- Pour the mixture into prepared jars, cover when cold.

Best kept for 2 -3 months, but I eat it straight away or give it away. If you decorate the jars it makes a lovely present.

Stick to the basic weights, you can make many combinations of chutney. Make it up with season's fruits and gifts of nature.

Basic Stuff

Pastry

Pastry making is one of those simple basic skills which is an essential kitchen art – fortunately the best way of making good pastry is just that – simple and basic, and I have set out here the ways which I have found to be most successful for me. It is very much a guide rather than a definitive way of doing things – finding good variations are part of the fun of cooking.

The number of pastry recipes included here are more than I originally intended, but my friends kept saying, "please include this and that", so I hope it's not a bore to people who don't eat pastry.

The types of pastry I have offered you are:

Plain Shortcrust - it has many uses both for sweet and savoury dishes. The taste and texture changes as to the different shortenings used; also whether you use an egg yoke or sugar or gluten-free flour.

Flaky Pastry - I suppose this is the one I use the most, again for both sweet and savoury. I'm constantly making it and have it on hand in the freezer; but good frozen flaky pastry is now available in the supermarkets.

Hot Water-Crust - I know full well it is a little difficult to make, but well worth having a go at. Don't try it if you are a little stressed; you need to play very soothing music not heavy metal!

Gluten-Free - if you have friends who are coeliac they will be most impressed if you make them pastry using gluten-free flour.

Because it is time-consuming to make, always make more than you need and divide it up, saving the remainder in the freezer. It is worth the effort because it is so much nicer than anything you will buy in the shops.

Plain Shortcrust

Ingredients

1lb (455g)   plain flour

10oz (285g) Cookeen / butter / lard of your choice (the shortening)

Pinch of Salt

water to mix

1tsp icing sugar   Yes I really do mean this; it makes the pastry very "short" and a lovely colour.

Rubbing in Method

- Rub shortening into the flour, with salt, icing sugar, and enough water to mix to soft dough.
- Roll out and decide if you want to make traditional pastie shapes using a saucer or roll it long and cut into squares or triangles. I make a different shape depending on the fillings.

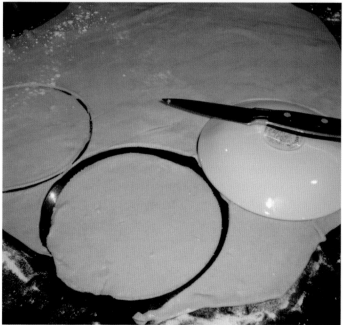

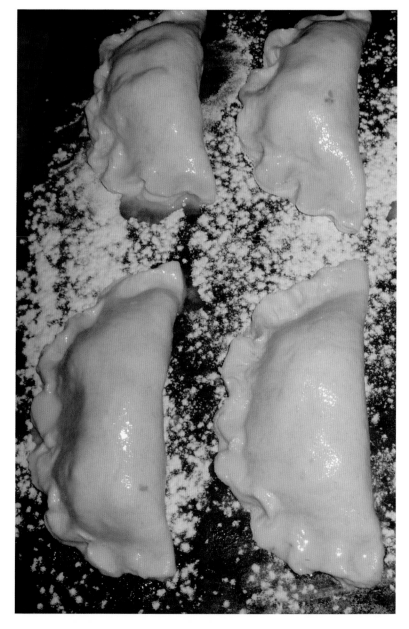

Flaky Pastry

Ingredients

1lb (455g)	plain flour
8oz (225g)	best butter
8oz (225g)	lard or Cookeen
1 tsp	icing sugar
1 tsp	salt
10fl oz (300ml)	cold water and the juice of 1/2 lemon

Rubbing in Method

- Put the flour, icing sugar and the salt into a bowl. Divide the fats into four portions (two of butter, two of fat) ; rub one portion – either the fat or the butter – into the flour and mix to a firm dough with the cold water. The amount of water varies with different kinds of flour.

- Knead the dough lightly until smooth, then roll out an oblong. Put a second portion of fat in small pieces onto 2/3 of the dough. Fold in three, half turn the dough to bring the open edge towards you and roll out again to an oblong. Put on a third portion of fat in small pieces, fold dough in three, wrap in cling film and put in fridge for ½ hour.

- Roll out the dough again, put on the remaining fat in pieces, fold and roll as before. The pastry is now ready to use as required.

Hearty and Wholesome Stuff

Traditional Country Pasties

In praise of the humble Pastie, there's nowt in t'world as tastie.

Ingredients

Pastry	1lb of your choice
12 oz (340g)	lean beef cut into small pieces
1 onion	peeled and finely chopped
2 carrots	peeled and finely chopped (also add a little swede if liked)
2 potatoes	peeled and chopped
salt and pepper	
3tbs good stock	
1 egg	to make the egg wash

Method

- In a bowl, combine all these ingredients.
- Roll out the pastry and use a saucer to make as many round shapes as you can and fill them with the mixture.
- Brush one half of the pastie with the beaten egg wash and bring together pressing lightly. Fold the edges over working towards you from one end to the other. Repeat until all the filling is used.
- Place on baking tray and cook in a pre-heated oven for approximately 1 hour at 200C (400F, Gas 6). After ½ hour, turn down to 175C (350F, Gas 4).

When I say baking tray - that's what I mean. Why! If you use a flat sheet you'll find out why. Most pasties, no matter how hard you try to seal them, nearly always leak, leaving mess in the oven, which is definitely not what is wanted.

These pasties can also be made with lamb, or cold minced lamb from the joint, and also with cooked minced beef.

Cheese, Onion and Spinach Pastie

Ingredients

Pastry	1lb of your choice
12 oz (340g)	grated cheese (Cheddar is good)
12 oz (240g)	onions peeled and sliced (either fried gently in butter or boiled in a little milk and then drained)

salt and pepper

1 bag spinach   Wilt this in a little butter

1 egg to make the egg wash

Method

- Mix the cheese, onion and spinach together in a bowl.
- Roll out the pastry, decide what shape you require and fill as previously described.
- Cook for 20 to 30 minutes in a hot oven (200C, 400F, Gas 6).
- Instead of doing individual shapes, you can make this on a plate the old-fashioned way if you prefer, or make one big slab and cut in pieces, as illustrated.

Cheese and Onion Pastie

Ingredients

Pastry	1lb of your choice
12 oz (340g)	grated cheese (Cheddar is good)
12 oz (340g)	onions peeled and sliced (either fried gently in butter or boiled in a little milk and then drained, keep the liquid for the sauce)

salt and pepper

4 oz butter (115g)

4 large tbs flour

3/4 pint (15 fl oz, 426ml) milk made up from the liquid above and topped up as required

1 egg	to make the egg wash

Method

- Melt the butter in a large saucepan, add the flour, and make to a paste.
- Add the milk, bring to the boil, then turn down to simmer, stir continuously to make a very thick sauce. Beat to make it creamy.
- Take it off the heat and add salt and pepper and a teaspoon of mustard if you like. Now stir in cheese and onion and put to one side to cool.
- Cook in pre heated oven 200C (400F, Gas 6) for 30 minutes turn down for a further 20 minutes approximately.

Again these can be made as individual pasties, but if I'm catering for large numbers then I double both the quantities of pastry and filling. I cut the pastry into two and roll out half, make an oblong or square and place on baking tray. Place a series of large tablespoons of the filling on the pastry - leaving spaces between which are egg-washed. The other half of the pastry is rolled to the same size and put on top. The edges need to be pressed around the fillings to seal them in a grid, but be careful not to puncture the pastry. You will probably end up with 16 – 20 pasties but made and baked as a whole. It's like one big slab of pastie – I hope you understand. Then you can cut the slab into individual pieces and serve them hot with jacket potatoes and salad, or have a picnic and eat them cold.

This recipe is something I have tried to replicate from Davy's in Fargate, Sheffield in the fifties and sixties. The shop was renowned for its pasties, pastries and beautiful cakes, and was the meeting place for many. It was the forerunner of the coffee shops and delis of today.

Mushroom and Onion Pastie

Ingredients

Pastry   1lb of your choice

12 oz (340g) mushrooms, sliced and cooked in a little butter

12 oz (240g) onions peeled and sliced (either fried gently in butter or boiled in a little milk and then drained; keep the liquid for the sauce)

salt and pepper

4 oz   butter (115g)

4 large tbs   flour

3/4 pint (15 fl oz 436ml) milk made up from the liquid above and topped up as required (use a little cream to make it special)

1 egg   to make the egg wash

Method

- Make exactly the same way as for the cheese and onion.

Salmon, Spinach and Cream Cheese Packets or Parcels

Ingredients

Pastry	1lb of your choice
4 salmon fillets	lightly poached in milk for approx 5 mins
1 bag spinach	either cooked in the microwave or wilt in a pan with a little butter or olive oil
2 sweet onions	peeled and chopped and gently cooked in a little butter
Salt and pepper	
large pkt cream cheese	
1 egg	to make the egg wash

Beautiful if eaten straight from the oven for lunch or as a starter; just as wonderful for picnics or parties.

Method

- Place the salmon in a bowl, first making sure you have taken out all the bones and removed the skin. Gently flake the fish by hand (I always use my hands, but if you feel more comfortable use a spoon or fork to do this process), then add the spinach, onion, salt and pepper, and the cream cheese.
- Next, roll out the pastry in a square or oblong depending on how big your parcels are to be. Cut out the required amount, place the fish mixture in centre, wet the edges with the egg wash, crimp up the edges and place on a baking tray.
- Cover the top with egg wash, sprinkle a little sea salt on top, and bake for 20 – 25 minutes in a hot oven until lovely and golden brown.

Vegetable Pastie

Ingredients

Pastry	1lb of your choice
2 large tomatoes	chopped
1 sweet onion	sliced and cooked in oil or butter (or you can use red onion)
1 pepper	de-seeded and diced (any colour)
2 courgettes	chop up finely
2 to 3 oz	butter or olive oil
Salt and pepper	
1 egg	to make the egg wash

Method

- Melt the butter or oil in a pan and fry the onions until golden. Put to one side in a small bowl.
- Melt a little more butter/olive oil and do the same with the peppers. Likewise, repeat for the courgettes and the tomatoes, or drizzle with olive oil and roast in the over, as in picture opposite.
- Roll out the pastry into the shapes required, and spoon in the vegetable filling. Wet the edges with the egg wash, crimp up the edges and place on a baking tray.
- Put in pre-heated oven (200C, 400F, Gas 6) for approx 30 minutes or until lovely and golden.

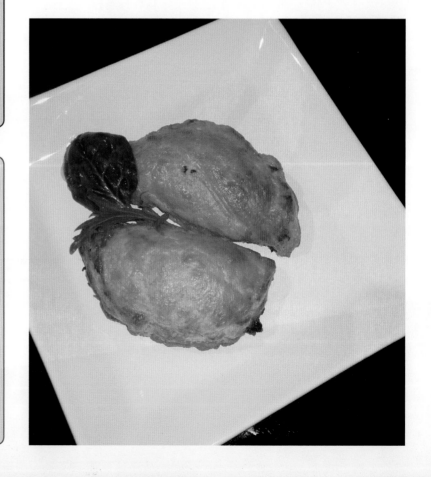

Easy Stuff

Plain Flan

Ingredients

8oz (225g)	flaky pastry
1 large	sweet onion peeled, chopped and fried in a little butter until pale gold
6	rashers bacon use streaky smoked bacon, lightly grill and cut into pieces
4oz (115g)	Cheddar cheese grated
Salt and pepper	
A shake of mixed herbs	
4	fresh eggs
10 fl oz (275ml) single cream	

Method

- Pre heat the oven
- Roll out the pastry and line a suitably sized greased flan dish
- Put in the bacon, onion, grated cheese
- Take the eggs and beat well together with the cream and the seasoning
- Pour over the filling and bake in a hot oven 200C (400F, Gas 6) for 15 – 20 minutes. Then turn down the oven to 175C (350F, Gas 4) and cook for a further 20 minutes until golden brown and has a 'soft set" to the finger touch. Don't burn your fingers – my sore finger is well practised.

This is included as a special request from Kim's dear friend Kate. It is one of the easiest recipes to make. Fraser made this one, took the photograph while Granny was in the way trying to make plum chutney – hence the still-life arrangement of plums and apples around the beautifully presented flan in the photo opposite.

Student Stuff

Basic Chicken and Vegetable Pie

This is for my young student friends at University, with the emphasis on a reasonably easy meal to prepare, which can be shared with their fellow students. Perfect for those beginning of term gatherings.

Ingredients

pkt of 6 basic Chicken breasts cut into pieces

4 to 6 carrots   peeled and sliced

2 onions   peeled and sliced thinly

Approx ½ pint (10 fl oz, 284ml) stock

½ pint (10 fl oz, 284ml)   milk

2oz (55g)   butter or cooking oil

2 large tbs   flour

Salt and pepper

A bunch of herbs, if available, parsley is the best

4 tbs double cream if budget will allow

8oz (225g)   button mushrooms wiped and sliced
                    (optional)

8oz (225g)   quantity of pastry

Method

- Melt half the butter in a large saucepan, and gently fry the chicken breasts for 8 to 10 minutes, stirring occasionally. Take out the breasts and place in a dish and leave to one side.

- Using the same saucepan, melt the remaining butter and lightly fry the onions, carrots, and mushrooms for approximately 8 minutes, stirring form time to time. Add the herbs and the seasoning, stir in the flour and cook for 2 minutes.

- Next, gradually add the milk and the stock, and stir continuously until the sauce comes to the boil and thickens and is smooth. Then simmer for a further 3 minutes.

- Add the chicken pieces, gently stir in and cook for a further 10 minutes on a very low heat.

- Now, put the filling into a deep pie dish, and allow to cool before you put the pastry on top .

- Either make your own pastry, or buy a packet. Roll out the pastry on a lightly floured surface. Make it large enough to cover the top of the dish with a bit spare.

- Cover the chicken, trim off the extra and use this to make a decoration on the top. Brush with milk to glaze, and put in preheated oven to bake at 200C (400F, gas mark 6) for 20 minutes. lower the oven temperature to 180C (360F, Gas 5) and cook for a further 30 minutes or until golden brown.

Last job – after you have put the chicken pie in the oven, peel the potatoes, put into saucepan with boiling water, 1/2 teaspoon of salt and cook until tender – approx 20 minutes. Drain and mash until smooth, add butter and milk and beat them with a fork to make them fluffy.

By this time your fellow students will either be breathing down your neck or have gone to the pub for a pint and a pastie. Good luck, and hope you don't have to do the washing-up.

I recently made a trial run with this recipe using 10 chicken breasts (pro rata the rest) – and added sliced par-boiled potatoes and peas. This made three complete pies – enough to feed 14 hungry mouths after a long walk, at a cost of under £15 – or £1 per portion. Not a bad costing for when planning your economy!

Summer-time meadow

You never know who might drop in

Historical Stuff

Charlotte Brontë, Jane Eyre, and Hathersage.

"I turned in the direction of the sound, and there amongst the romantic hills, whose changes and aspect I had ceased to note an hour ago, I saw a hamlet and a spire. All the valley at my right hand was full of pasture fields, and corn fields, and woods, and a glittering stream ran zig-zag through the varying shades of green."

This was how Charlotte Brontë in her novel 'Jane Eyre' describes the heroine's first sight of the village of Morton after her attention is drawn to it by the sound of the church clock striking, and might very well have been the view seen on the previous two pages. The fictitious village of Morton is undoubtedly our village of Hathersage, and many of the episodes and places described in the book can be identified with locations in and around Hathersage, which she knew well.

Charlotte's school friend Ellen Nussey was the sister of the Henry Nussey who was Vicar of Hathersage from 1845 to 1847. In 1839 Charlotte refused a proposal of marriage from Henry (he made it by letter rather than in person!), which is perhaps not surprising as it seems he was something of a sententious and frigid prig. He eventually did find someone who agreed to marry him and it was while he and his bride were on honeymoon that Ellen was joined by Charlotte on Thursday 26th June 1845, to prepare the Vicarage for the return of the vicar and his bride. During her three-week stay in the Vicarage she walked up to the moors and visited many of the houses round about, absorbing the atmosphere, meeting people and seeing places that were to reappear in a different guise within the narrative of 'Jane Eyre'.

In the book, Hathersage is renamed as 'Morton', possibly because when Jane arrived in the village by stage-coach and alighted at 'The George', the local post house, she would most likely have been greeted by the landlord who at the time was a Mr Morton.

The very name 'Eyre' was and still is a well-known surname in the area, with many Eyre family graves in the church-yard and church itself – one particular branch of the family having been Lords of the Manor for over 800 years. Not far from the Vicarage is the imposing North Lees Hall, which was occupied at that time by a Mary Eyre, a widow with four unmarried children. It is widely believed that North Lees became the model for Thornfield Hall in the novel – 'thorn' being an anagram of 'north', and 'lea' is an old English word for a field.

But there is other more substantial evidence given in the author's description of Thornfield. After Jane's first night in residence there she got up early and went out into the grounds: *'It was a fine autumn morning . . . I looked up and surveyed the front of the mansion. It was three stories high, of proportions not vast, though considerable: a gentleman's manor house not a nobleman's seat: battlements round the top gave it a picturesque look. Its grey front stood out well from the background of the rookery . . . Further off were the hills, not so lofty as those around Lowood, nor so craggy . . . but yet quiet and lonely hills enough.'*

Jane later goes out 'onto the leads', up a very narrow staircase to the attics and thence by a ladder and *'through a trap door to the roof of the hall. I was now on a level with the crow colony, and could see into their nests.'*

These descriptions fit North Lees exactly. Perhaps it is significant too that the first mistress of North Lees, Agnes Ashurst, is reputed to have become demented and was confined to a room on the second floor where the walls were padded for her protection.

There are other parallels – Moor House, the home of the Rev St John Rivers, has strong similarities to Moorseats House, and the character of Rivers himself is similar to the descriptions we have of Henry Nussey. The site of the village school, of which Rivers asks Jane to be the schoolmistress, also fits the location of the old Greer Green school near Thorpe Farm; although the building itself has now disappeared it was fully functioning when Charlotte Brontë visited in 1845.

North Lees Hall in 1924; it would not be much different from when Charlotte Brontë visited in 1845. Many of the windows were still blocked up from the 'window tax' days.

Left – a water-colour of 1881 of the bridge over the Hood Brook at Hathersage. The tall building to the right was originally a baker's shop but is now the site of the present butcher's shop. In 'Jane Eyre', Jane exchanges a pair of gloves for some bread at the baker's shop at the bottom of the village in 'Morton' after her night on the moors; perhaps this was the very building the author used as the model. Beyond on the left of the picture is the original George Hotel building where Charlotte Brontë would have alighted from her coach, just 36 years before this picture was painted.

The Misses Hodgkinson

The two pictures opposite are of the Hathersage WI in the 1930s; I think they must have been celebrating their 21st Birthday.

The lady in prominent position by the cake in both photographs is Miss Enid Hodgkinson of Moorseats (my Godmother). She was WI President for many years and was a leading light in the WI country-wide. She had many other interests and obsessions, one of which being the reading of plays – yes – she read vast numbers of them, often reading the same one over and over again; there were times she didn't go to bed and would read on into the night, only to be found still fast asleep in her chair at noon.

Other of her obsessions were Charlotte Brontë, which I'll tell you about another time, and Clarnico Peppermint Creams. Many was the time I had to run down to Fred Ramsden's grocery shop in the village to buy them for her, and also to enquire how many boxes Fred had left, and request that he re-order if the number was low.

Winter afternoons were spent on very large jigsaws which she pieced together on the big dining room table which had a very thick cover and could be rolled back over the jigsaw to keep it in place when she had had enough. She would get very cross if her younger sister, Miss Monica, invited the local MP for a meal, and especially if her unfinished puzzle was disturbed by it. She clearly enjoyed giving Miss Monica a telling off, and enjoyed giving me one even more.

As well as reading plays she was also sometimes involved in their performance; I'm not sure what her involvement was in the 1950s village production of Jane Eyre, but I do know that most of the props were borrowed from Moorseats and she persuaded Lol Holmes to borrow a suitable van to transport them to the village hall where the performance was to take place. Mo made many of the ladies' dresses, and we still had them in the prop box in the loft for many years after.

Because of the local interest in 'Jane Eyre' we young children were allowed to watch a performance, but only because Mrs Kirby, who played Mrs Fairfax, was there to keep an eye on us. It was our very first introduction to a stage play and we talked about it for ages afterwards. Some of the older girls of 14 or 15 'fell in love with' Mr Rochester who was played by Jim Taylor, and the character of Jane herself was played by Phyllis Ramsden. It was so romantic because the two of them really did fall in love, married, and had two daughters, one of whom, Becky Winstanley, is still very much involved in our drama group in the village.

The three Miss Hodgkinson's did their best to calm my native instincts. Miss Monica loved nature and taught me so many interesting facts and things about wildflowers, animals and birds. They were our Moorseats neighbours till 1978.

Miss Enid was of the firm belief that Charlotte Bronte did actually come and take tea at Moorseats in 1845. Very occasionally she allowed the Bronte Society to visit, of course they took tea. It was always made into a special event. I knew my place; I had to provide homemade refreshments under her supervision. People sat around reading passages from Jane Eyre, which I thought was great fun.

Miss Monica always had a car and drove (very badly and couldn't reverse – a bit like I am now) but latterly she'd say to me 'Now Mary, could you just take me somewhere'. One day she said 'Mary would you take me to Broomhill? I've got to see Claude Price because I want a new suit.' So I said 'Yes, Miss Monica'. We set off, up the dale to Stanage, and she said 'Stop. Stop the car.' So we stopped and looking out and she said 'Isn't that absolutely wonderful?' It was the middle of October and the colours were glorious. Off we went to Claude Price at Broomhill. 'Good morning Miss Monica, how are you?' She hit him on the back and said 'Claude, I'm champion. I want you to make me a suit the colour of the moors at twelve o'clock today.' And he said 'You'll mean the Donegal Tweed, Miss Monica.' 'Something like that' she said 'A bit of heather, a bit of bracken and a bit of sludge.'

Days Gone By

Late on a summer's evening,
In a sun-kissed Derbyshire dale,
In a cool, stone farmhouse kitchen,
I sat drinking strong brown ale.

Golden rays poured in through the doorway,
And the shadows grew long by my feet,
And the dogs grinned up from the flagstones
As the day lost some of its heat.

The warm dusk crept round the corner
Like a velvet thief in the night,
As the sun sank over the hillside,
Blazing bronze, in the fading light.

I rose and walked to the doorway,
And looked across to the tor,
Where the sky was shot with orange and gold,
Blending into the purple moor.

The moon rose over the orchard,
I could smell the new-mown hay,
And time stood still in the twilight,
At the end of a perfect day.

John Stocks, 1992

The church decorated for Harvest Festival in the 1930s. I know that my Granny Mary would have made a big contribution to this decoration and Uncle Roly would have grown many of the plants.

Church Harvest flowers 2011 were organised by Jane Marsden, and the altar flowers were arranged by today's Granny Mary. Young blood is required to continue the tradition of decorating our wonderful old church at Festive times and throughout the year. Volunteers, please.

Harvest Stuff

Rabbit Pie

Why have I included Rabbit Pie? Because it was an important ingredient of my personal past and part of the social history of my village. To my vegetarian friends I do apologise.

Rabbit was our staple diet at the farm when I was a little girl. Rabbits were a plenty and Asa, our local butcher, would take as many as possible as meat was still on ration well in to the 1950's. Rabbit was the most popular, cheap and easily available meat. My Father, who knew well that certain chaps came poaching on the land, later said in the 1960's – "far better to have the honest local poacher than the evil myxomatosis", a rabbit disease which was introduced and spread by man. In my view, this was the main reason for rabbit going out of fashion; 40 years on, I now believe there is a resurgence of rabbit on the menu in the UK.

Ingredients

8oz (225g) quantity of pastry

1 lb (455g) of rabbit meat cubed or diced

4 rashers of smoked streaky bacon, cut into strips

2 to 3 carrots, peeled and diced

2 onions, peeled and finely sliced

1 tbsp of chopped fresh parsley

1 tsp of finely chopped fresh sage (use dried if fresh not available)

1 pinch of freshly grated nutmeg

2 tbsp of flour

Salt and pepper

6 dried apricots or prunes - chopped (optional)

Approx 1 pint (570ml) of stock . . . rabbit or chicken

1 egg to glaze

Method

- You will require a deep 3 pint (1.7 litre) pie dish.
- Place the rabbit in the dish, add the flour and salt and pepper. With your fingers roll the rabbit into the flour until it is all lightly dusted.
- Put the bacon strips on top, then the vegetables, the dried fruit, and the herbs.
- Lastly pour over the stock, making sure it is no more than 3/4 of the way up the dish. Dampen the rim of the dish with water.
- Roll out your pastry on a floured board, making sure it is larger than the top of the dish. cut a strip approx 1 inch wide and line the dampened outer edge of the rim. Next put the pastry lid on, and trim. If any pastry is left, make rabbit decorations for the top.
- Brush with egg glaze and bake in a pre heated oven at 200C (400F, Gas 6) for 30 minutes.
- Remove from the oven, cover with foil, and cook for a further 1 hour at 170C (325F, Gas 3).

Pheasant or Mixed Game Crumble

Ingredients

Small Pk	dried mixed berries, cranberries or chestnuts
4	pheasant breasts or 1 kg mixed game
4	rashers smoked bacon
½ pint (284ml)	stock (made from rest of bird or stock recipe)
2	sweet onions
1tsp	horseradish
3oz (85g)	butter
½ pint (284ml)	red wine or stock
½ pint (284mls)	cream
	salt and pepper

Method

- Brown the bacon and meat in a thick pan into which you have melted the butter and browned the onions. Shake the pan about for a bit.
- Add the stock and season well. Cook gently in oven for 30 minutes; stir half way through cooking.
- Pour in cream mixed with horseradish and mixed fruit and cook for a further 15 minutes.
- Now, if you wish to eat this without the crumble on top just as a plain pheasant casserole then that is fine. Cook for approximately 15 minutes longer.

The Crumble

Ingredients

8oz (225g)	whole meal, brown flour, plain flour or mixed
4oz (115g)	oatmeal
8oz (225g)	butter (my granny used dripping for this)! good pinch of salt
4oz (115g)	coarsely ground hazelnuts, almonds or walnuts

Method

- Place flour, oatmeal and salt into a bowl and rub in the butter till it resembles breadcrumbs.
- Put cooked meat into a high sided dish, cover with crumble mix and scatter the chopped nuts over the top.
- Dot with a little butter.
- Bake in oven 200C (400F, Gas 6) for 15 minutes turn down to 170C (325F, Gas 3) and cook for a further 10 – 20 minutes until golden brown and crunchy on top. Serve with creamy mashed potatoes, lovely green vegetables and red cabbage.

Caution: don't get your oven too hot like I did or you might burn your nuts.

Pots and Stuff

A Derbyshire-born potter, Geoff Fuller lives and works at the 'Three Stags Heads', a 17th century pub at the ancient cross-roads of Wardlow Mires near Foolow, where once stood the last gibbet to be used in Derbyshire.

Geoff and his wife Pat work at their pottery during the week, but become landlord and lady of the pub at weekends. The finest of draught ales are available in the stone-flagged bar of the Three Stags, as well as excellent food cooked on the premises, served on their own crocks and often featuring locally caught game. Just try their rabbit and chocolate pie – wow!

Geoff's pots are world renowned; as well as his famous figures, he produces traditional style slipware, dishes, mugs and jugs which have the look and feel of medieval vessels – many decorated with his much loved motifs of foxes, dogs, sheep, pigs, chickens, hares and owls.

I just love it, and on the next few pages I have used Geoff's pots 'on location' in his studio at the Three Stags Heads to show off some of the pies and pasties made from recipes in this book. Pies are made and eaten – a passing pleasure – but Geoff's pots, of which I have a small collection, are a joy for ever.

Studio photographs by Simon Bull. See more of Geoff Fuller's work at www.geofffullerpottery.co.uk.

Showing how Granny Mary's pies are the perfect complement to the Fuller figures, mugs and dishes

Party Baked Ham

Ingredients

3 – 4kg piece of ham from Chatsworth Farm Shop.

I know it's a bit expensive but its beautiful meat and specially cured and has a magnificent flavour.

Method

- Place in a large roasting tin in a preheated oven –190C, 375F, Gas 5; put a little cider in the bottom of the tin and spoon glaze over the top, and keep basting while cooking. I use a meat thermometer to 71C. It takes 25 minutes pr kg to cook fully. Let it rest for 30 minutes before you slice.

This is my extravagance when we are entertaining or having a large family gathering. It will serve 20 easily and is wonderful cold in sandwiches. We serve it with the peas and spinach, red cabbage and mashed creamed potatoes, sweet potatoes and parsnips – Cumberland or Cranberry sauce.

Peas and Spinach

Ingredients

1lb (455g) bag	frozen petit pois
Large bag	spinach
4 sprays	mint leaves taken off and chopped
6 – 8 tbs	Kalamata extra virgin oil
	sea salt and black pepper
2tbs	caster sugar

Method

- Bring a large pan of water to boil with ½ sugar and a teaspoon of salt, put in peas and simmer for a few minutes till tender, drain and leave on side.
- Next cook spinach in perhaps 3 batches. Put a tablespoon of oil in a large frying pan over a high heat stir fry until wilted. Cook remainder the same way.
- Whizz half of the peas with a hand blender and a little of the olive oil.
- Finally mix the pureed peas with the cooked peas and spinach in a large bowl, add seasoning, sugar and mint leaves and the last of the olive oil – it is now ready to serve.

I make this a day before it saves time if it's to be used for a party. Just heat up in microwave, Serves 8 – 12. Freezes well.

Red Cabbage Bake

Ingredients

5 tbs	red wine vinegar
2lb (900g)	red cabbage trimmed, cored and thinly sliced
2 large	sweet onions peeled and sliced
5fl oz (142ml)	red wine or port
2	apples peeled, cored and thinly sliced
2tbs	brown sugar
Pkt	dried cranberries
	salt and pepper
	olive oil
3tbs	redcurrant jelly
Grated nutmeg	
Grated orange rind	

Method

You will need a heavy pan with a lid.

- Heat the oil over medium heat and fry onions for 5 minutes till golden, stir in the apples and cook for a further 3 – 4 minutes until they are soft.
- Add the red cabbage, red wine vinegar, sugar, red wine and seasoning, orange rind and nutmeg. Bring to the boil stirring from time to time.
- Cover and place in preheated oven 160C (310F, Gas 3) for approximately 1½ hours. The cabbage should be tender and the liquid absorbed, stir occasionally. Add a little more wine if pan goes dry before the cabbage has cooked.
- Add the cranberries towards the end of the cooking time.
- Just before serving stir in redcurrant jelly – rest.
- Reheat in dish on top of stove or microwave when required.

I also make this the day before needed; it does actually taste better with a rest.

Roasted Almonds – Flathers family recipe

Ingredients

Packet of whole blanched almonds

Amount of special olive oil

– Greek Kalamata Extra Virgin OO is best

Sea salt

Method

- Simply put oil in heavy bottom frying pan, get it reasonably hot.
- Put in almonds and keep stirring don't let them burn – beware.
- Place double sheet of kitchen roll on work surface.
- Place almonds on kitchen roll and shake in salt.
- When they are cold put into screw top jars.

If you are using 1 pk of almonds you'll need 1 tbs of oil.

Wonderful eaten straight from the pan – your friends will love them.

Mary and Hannah

Michael and I were really thrilled when Hannah Hawxwell came to stay in 1993, and we loved her. She was the most wonderful lady I ever met and at the height of her fame, and was about to be whisked off to the States on the QE2, having just returned from a trip to Venice.

On her arrival I apologised for our place not being 'posh' like the place she stayed at in Venice, but she paid us the biggest compliment saying that our home suited her way of life far more, and she wanted to stay for a lot longer and go up on the moors above us with Becky the spaniel who also became very attached to her.

We kept in touch for a time and when we were organising a fund-raising event for the Hathersage Players she said, in her beautifully apt English, "I'll look upon it favourably to help you," and she did.

Why do I mention Hannah Hawxwell? I was looking at some photographs the other day and came across the one below of me tending a couple of our sheep. A friend who was visiting at

the time said, "Mary, you're getting more and more like Hannah Hawxwell." Far from being upset I took it as a great compliment, for I couldn't think of a better person to be compared with.

When Hannah was staying with us I wanted to adopt her as my new 'official' Granny, but decided that this would be inappropriate when I discovered that she was only seventeen years older than me. I hope I grow old as gracefully and beautifully as she has done – well into her 80s now, and no longer living in her famous hill-top farm but in the village, surrounded by her familiar 'stuff'.

Trifling Stuff

Trifle

I'm sure every family has their own special recipe for trifle. This is very simple, I've made this for as many as 50+ for Teddy Bears Picnic parties and there was never enough.

Sadly we had to discontinue our Teddy Bears Picnic days, which were wonderfully happy occasions. But in these times of Health & Safety legislation our garden is perhaps seen as having too many trips and traps for little adventurers to play in with total safety. A shame because there should be a bit of adventure even in small children's lives provided that the risks are properly assessed and the parents made aware of them. Kids love an adventure garden that's got a bit of a challenge about it; if they never learn how to cope with a little risk then how will they learn the boundaries between what is safe and what isn't.

Back to trifle before I get carried away on another hobby horse!

This recipe makes a bowl of trifle for 8. I always make a bit more as I love it for breakfast.

Ingredients

Large	Swiss roll
¾ jar	either raspberry or strawberry jam
	a 'Communion' of fortified wine, sherry, Madeira or sweet liquor (optional)
1½pts (30 fl oz, 900ml)	of home made custard
½pt (10 fl oz, 300ml)	whipping cream
1 Punnet	Raspberries

Method

- Take Swiss roll and chop up roughly, place in a bowl.
- Put the jar of jam (with the sherry - if used) into the microwave. Make sure you put the jar into a bowl because if it gets too hot it bubbles over and makes a mess. It needs to get very hot to dissolve the jam. Careful how you take it out … or it will burn you.
- Pour the jam over the Swiss roll; you can put ½ the raspberries, or any other fruit for that matter, in the bottom – it's up to you. Make sure jam mixture covers sponge, and then leave to cool.
- Add the made quantity of custard, and finally put the whipped cream on top, and decorate with the remaining raspberries.

Custard for Trifle

Ingredients

1pt (20 fl oz, 600ml)   full fat milk

½pt (10 fl oz, 300ml)   cream

6   egg yolks

4tbs   sugar

2 tsp   cornflour

1 vanilla pod or 1 tsp of vanilla
                              extract

Method

- Firstly, rinse your pan out in cold water . . . why? – it's so the milk and cream don't stick to the bottom.
- Put the milk and the cream in the pan, add the vanilla pod with the seeds scraped out (or the vanilla extract) and bring to just under the boil.
- Meanwhile beat the egg yokes and sugar in a large bowl until they are very pale and beautifully creamy. Add the cornflour at the end of the beating.
- Now pour a small amount of the hot liquid into the creamed mixture and lightly beat it, keep adding a little more, until it's all mixed in.
- Pour it all back into the pan on a low heat, and continually whisk with a balloon whisk until it is thick and cooked. It can take several minutes, but do not overcook . . . unless you want runny scrambled eggs!
- Put to one side and cool if it's for trifle. If it's for other puddings, you can use straight away, pour into a jug or lock the kitchen door and get a spoon!

The Bakewell Pudding –

Granny Mary's Bakewell Pudding

I have only ever written this recipe down once since I was 13. I was told to keep this simple run of numbers 1 – 6 in my head. My Granny said I was to keep it a 'secret.'

Many of her friends and relatives begged for it over the years but she never did tell as far as I know. Many of them tried to prise it out of me when I was young but I was not for giving. My intension was to give it to my daughter or at least show her how to make it.

So I've decided it's time finally to tell you all how to make my Granny's Bakewell Pudding. It's more about how to make it because everyone seems to know what goes in it (or so they think).

Ingredients

8oz quantity of flaky pastry

6oz (170gm)	granulated sugar
5	egg yolks
4oz (115g)	butter (melted not runny)
3tbs	strawberry jam
2tbs	ground almonds
1	egg white

One or two or you may say she has forgotten the almond essence. No I have not. If you want to add a few drops you can. Never buy or use flavouring, it's disgusting stuff – use proper extract.

Method

- First grease a deep baking dish. Take flakey pastry, roll out and line dish and spread jam on bottom.
- Separate 4 egg yolks into a big bowl along with 1 whole egg and the sugar.
- You now need to whisk for a long time until it's very thick and creamy.
- Add the melted butter and ground almonds, stir gently with a large spoon. Spread on top of jam.
- Bake in moderate oven 180C (360F, Gas 5) for 15 minutes, turn down to 170C (325F, Gas 3), cover if it's getting too brown, cook for 45 – 60 minutes. It will be soft set but when it goes cold it will be fine.

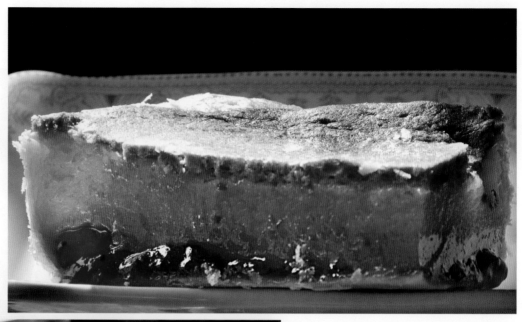

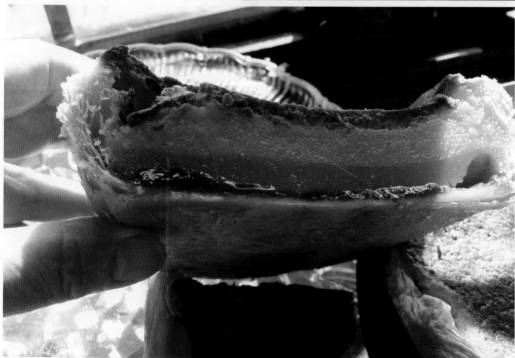

Bakewell's claim to fame is of course the famous pudding (not tart). Legend has it that is was created by accident in the kitchen of the White Horse coaching inn (which became the Rutland Arms in 1804) when the landlady, Mrs Greaves, gave the job of preparing a strawberry tart to an inexperienced assistant. Although she got the ingredients right the method she used was totally wrong, and what came out of the oven wasn't a strawberry tart but the first Bakewell pudding. Nowadays, during the summer season, over 12,000 puddings are sold each week, so Mrs Greaves's inexperienced cook has a lot to answer for. And it just shows that sometimes good things can happen when you don't follow the recipe.

As I have said, I have been making my Granny Mary's version of Bakewell pudding ever since she taught me her recipe, which she herself inherited from others even further back. I am making no claims that my recipe is the authentic one, but I know it is one that works, and is as simple as can be. Until now I have been true to my Granny M's request to keep it to myself, but I think she would understand that I have to pass it on to someone, otherwise it will disappear when I do.

Real Bakewell pudding made in the traditional way is a wonderfully special treat for those occasions when you want people to enjoy something a little different. It's not a pudding for everyday, but when you do have it people will remember and ask you for the recipe. You can pass it on if you wish, or keep it as your little secret, as given to you by Granny Mary.

Did Jane Austen ever taste a Bakewell Pudding?

There is strong evidence that in 1811 Jane Austen stayed at the Rutland Arms hotel in Bakewell while revising the manuscript of *Pride and Prejudice*, and may have used the interior of the inn as a setting for an important scene in the book. Elizabeth Bennett has arranged to meet the Darcys and Mr Bingley whilst staying at in the northern town of Lambton, which, as Jane Austen describes it, has many features in common with Bakewell. The Darcys are visiting Mr Bingley at nearby Pemberly, which, as described, has significant similarities to Chatsworth. Elizabeth is very apprehensive and discomforted in the anticipation of the meeting with BIngley, who has arrived separately, but:

'They had not been long together before Darcy told her that Bingley was also coming to wait on her; and she had barely time to express her satisfaction, and prepare for such a visitor, when Bingley's quick step was heard on the stairs, and in a moment he entered the room. All Elizabeth's anger against him had been long done away; but, had she still felt any, it could hardly have stood its ground against the unaffected cordiality with which he expressed himself on seeing her again.'

Later, in her room, Elizabeth lies awake for two hours, thinking about Mr. Darcy. It is here that she reads Jane's letter bearing news of Lydia's elopement with Mr. Wickham. Just as Elizabeth finishes reading, a servant admits Mr Darcy to the room and she tearfully shares with him her family's predicament. And the rest is literary history.

What I like is the idea of Jane Austen possibly tucking into a slice of Bakewell pudding, though ever so genteely, while imagining and writing this episode.

'Jane Austen' Letters

I happen to have a wonderful collection of 'cross-written' letters, most of them penned over a two-year period from 1814 to 1816 by William Bayldon to his intended, Mary Maw. This is the 'Jane Austen' period, and at that time it was the recipient of a letter rather than the sender who had to pay the postage, which was based on the size of the letter and the distance travelled – therefore the fewer pages used the less the cost. To use all the space available on the paper letters were cross-written, ie writing the equivalent of two sides on one side by turning the paper at 90 degrees and writing over the 'first' side.

Envelopes were not used as this would be an extra sheet of paper and would cost more for the recipient. The finished letter would be folded several times before being sealed with either sealing wax or a sealing wafer and the address added. Opposite is a photograph of part of one of the letters, and below a transcription of some of the content. I like the bit about measuring in 'nails'. A Nail was used for measuring cloth and was based on the length of the last two joints (including finger nail) of the middle finger – equivalent to 1/16 of a yard. I wonder what he wanted 'knobs' for?

Dated from Barnsley, 3rd month 14th day, 1815.

My dearest M.M.

Having a little leisure, or rather, not feeling disposed to begin work after so long a holiday, I think I cannot employ my time more pleasantly to myself than in assuring thee, not of my unabated, but increased attachment which every visit to G. tends to do, and always on leaving, for a day or two, feel uncomfortable at the separation, as I am always about to enjoy the society of my friends the most, when call'd upon by other ties to separate from them, being too much of that bashful disposition that requires a little time before I can possibly dissipate it, but which constant endeavours I am sure will overcome, agreeable to Bonaparte's advice to one of his Generals, we must let nothing but victory possess our minds, when we shall be sure to obtain it. I dare say thou wilt be surprized at this beginning, indeed, I appear to myself to be lead into it unaware tho' not unconscious of the necessity for it. I have executed thy commission of measuring the height of our rooms, they are 2 1/2 yards and 2 nails from the top of the moulding. I find we have no knobs that if thou wilt purchase them, I will repay thee when I have the happiness of seeing thee next, neither have I yet had the opportunity of purchasing a fender for the best room and if thou wilt not think this too much trouble and can meet with one to thy mind at Gainsbro: I shall tender thee my best thanks, (being all at present I can give thee) the width of the fireplace within (that is where the fender fits) is just a yard. I have looked through our Barnsley

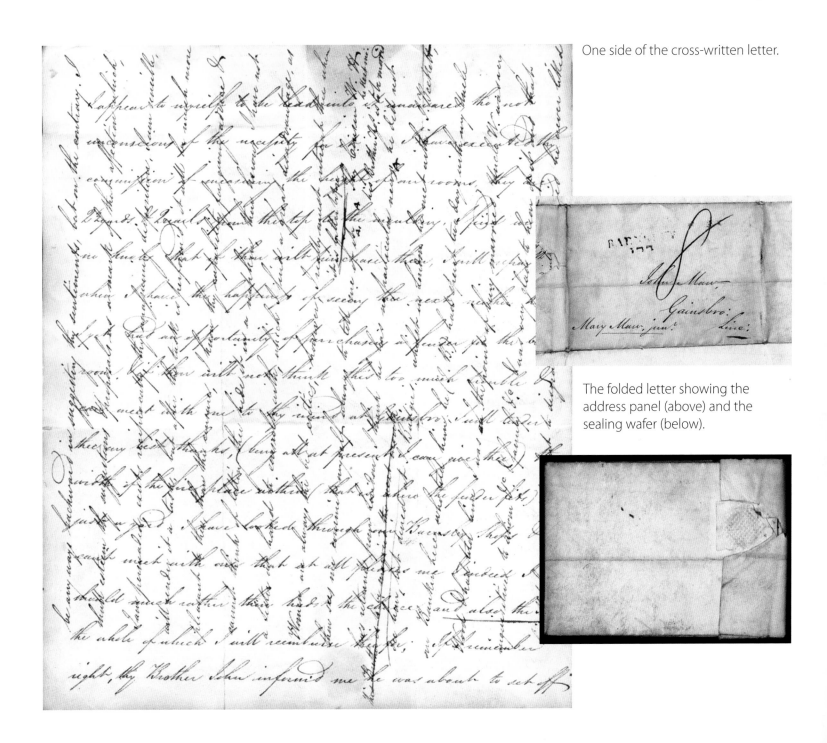

One side of the cross-written letter.

The folded letter showing the address panel (above) and the sealing wafer (below).

Chocolate Mousse

Simply the best according to my husband and family. Michael once said he could eat a bucket full, but I just can't afford to test him on that.

Ingredients

16oz (455g)	dark chocolate
8	eggs separated (need I say fresh, not from supermarket)
2 tbs	strong coffee dissolved in a little hot water
2 tbs	brandy

You will need 12 small wine glasses or it can be made in one glass bowl. Wine glasses do take up more shelf room in the fridge if you are catering for a party; I still prefer them though.

You are going to use a pan ½ full with water with a basin or bowl over the top. An important tip do not let the water do more than simmer, you don't want the boiling water to touch the bowl while the chocolate is being melted because it causes the chocolate to 'grain', so make sure there is plenty of space between and as soon as it's melted pull of heat to cool.

Method

- Melt the chocolate in the basin as described below left with the coffee; add brandy (if desired).
- When cool add the 8 egg yokes and beat together gently.
- Whisk the egg whites till very stiff, make sure you can tip them upside down over your head. If you couldn't you'll know what I mean next time.
- Very gently spoon and cut into the chocolate mixture making sure you don't see any egg whites.
- Spoon into glasses and place in fridge till required. Better made the day before you need to eat them. They keep for a few days but not in our house – word always gets round.

The Chocolate Mousse

Very Sweet Stuff

Meringues

Ingredients

1 fresh egg white + 2oz (55g) caster sugar

(Use this ratio to determine your desired amount)

I typically use 4 fresh egg whites, 8 oz caster sugar

Method

- This recipe takes a lot of beating so I would recommend that you use an electric mixer. Whisk up the egg whites until they are very stiff and you can turn the bowl upside down without the contents falling on your head. Now whip in ¼ of the sugar, beat this up again and repeat 3 more times.
- Prepare 2 or 3 large baking sheets with non-stick baking parchment and spoon on 24 to 30 meringues on each sheet.
- Put in oven at 110C (225F) for 3 hours until they are dry and golden.
- Store in tins until needed, put together with cream. These will keep in air tight tins for 2 to 3 weeks but do not freeze.

For special occasions I make these in several batches and store them until required. When catering for large parties, build them up into a pyramid and decorate with raspberries, strawberries and whatever takes your fancy!

Note: To avoid a disaster **you must**:

– make sure that no egg yolk escapes into the bowl.

– use clean grease-free bowl and whisk.

My friends tell me that gas ovens are not good for making meringues – I have no answer to this except find a friendly and accommodating neighbour with an electric oven!

Cheese Stuff

Three Tier Cheese Cake

by request from Victoria

Ingredients

Choose 3 rounds of different cheeses i.e.
Cheddar, Red Leicester and another white
cheese so you have shades of colour.

Collect ivy leaves, clean and dry and wipe with
a little oil. You can paint them with edible gold
paint or leave plain.

2 or 3 bunches of grapes (nice shape).

1 egg white whisked very soft with 2oz of icing
sugar (that's called frosting).

Method

- First put the largest cheese on the plate,
  then the second place this towards the back,
  put the last one on top so you have three
  tiers.
- Don't whisk the egg white frosting too early
  because it will run.
- An hour our two before you require the cake
  dip the bunches of grapes into egg white
  and drape on cheese in 3 curving swags.
- Decorate around with the ivy leaves just
  tuck in between cheeses.
- On the very top place a spray of roses or
  whatever flowers you choose. (Make sure
  they are not poisonous). My advice is to stick
  to the roses or use faux flowers.

To build this amazing structure you require a large strong round tray
or plate. Believe me, cheese is heavy.

Winter Wonderland

I remember the severe winters we had and the weather was always a challenge. My dad would walk into the kitchen with a lamb round his neck like a scarf and one under his arm, saying, "Will somebody find a bottle and get some milk?" He would set them down within the fender in front of the range, to my delight for as soon as I heard the bleat of a 'cade' lamb that needed a bit of love, then I was happy little girl.

Way back in 1947, the winter of the 'Big Snow' on the morning of 29th or 30th of January, Asa the butcher came up to kill a pig. How he walked up through thirteen foot snow drifts I'll never know, he was only 5 foot tall!

To get outside I had to be passed through the bedroom window because we couldn't open the doors with a 13ft drift of snow outside.

Mary and Andy, the hillside kids of 1947

Winters on the lane leading to Carr Head
can be interesting.

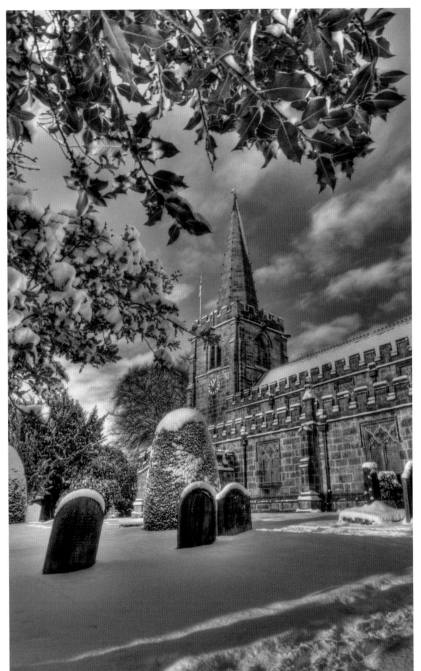

An old postcard view of 'Little John's Grave'.

Legend has it that Robin Hood's stalwart lieutenant, Little John, is buried in our ancient churchyard, and we still have his grave there to prove it! – and until the middle of the 18th century we also had his bow and cap hanging in the church, but these were removed some time in the 19th century to Cannon Hall in Yorkshire where the photo (right) of the bow was taken.

More important to me is the **fact** that my Granny Mary and her family are buried about twenty yards away from Little John's reputed resting place, just a little off to the left of the picture on the left – if you see what I mean.

Rustic Stuff

How to Make a Decorative 'Wood Tree'

Ingredients

First find a supply of old brass stair rods they are usually up to 18" (45cms) long. If you cannot find these, then improvise with any straight metal rods of a similar diameter and length.

A good chunky log with a flat bottom.

A drill bit and drill. This should be nominally the same diameter as the rod.

A poll parrot, this is a long handled wood cutting tool, like a big pair of secateurs.

Coppicing . . . in other words, go and find some suitable sticks – as in photo opposite.

Method

- First, prepare the base. Drill a hole in the top of the base approx 2"(5 cms) deep, and insert the rod making sure it is firm and a tight fit.
- Next you need to go and do a bit of coppicing; the tree we use is a Lime, but any wood will do as long as it is roughly the right size. Cut off sufficient pieces of approx 1"(2.5 cms) diameter, these will be cut to a more accurate length later.
- Now cut a 3" (7.5 cms) length of wood, and drill a hole vertically down the centre so it goes all the way through. You will need to drill from both sides. It should be held firmly in a vice whilst drilling. Thread this piece onto the rod and slide it all the way down to the bottom.
- Then cut a selection of the branches approx 1" (2½ cm) in diameter. You will require about 10 to 15 per tree (depending on the diameter and the length of the rod).
- Cut these pieces to different lengths, starting with 16"(40 cms) and progressively getting smaller in equal increments.
- Carefully drill a hole in the centre of each piece, and thread them onto the rod, one at a time, starting with the longest first.
- Continue to build them up until you get to 2" (5 cms) from the top of the rod. Spread the branches in different directions as you build it up.
- Cut another short piece, 3" (7.5 cms) long, and drill exactly as you did the short piece at the bottom.
- Finish by putting this on top.

Now you have a tree . . . I never thought I'd be able to explain how to do that – baking is much easier.

This tree, not made by us, is decorated in simple 'Shaker' style.

Naive Christmas tree

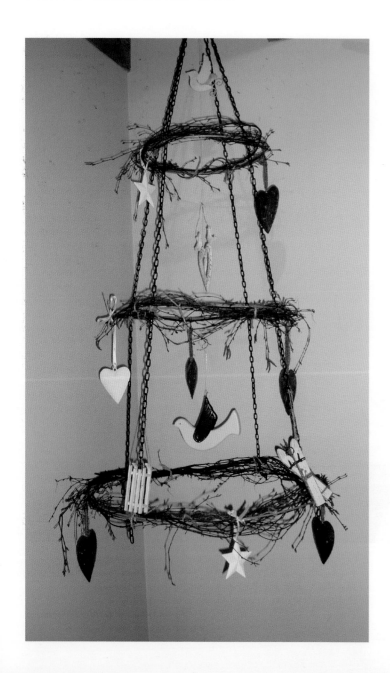

Every Christmas I try and concoct a new idea for a tree. This one has been much admired for it's simplicity. It is constructed from 3 rings made from fence wire, 4 lengths of chain, string to tie it all together, and weeping birch wrapped around the rings. Decorate in any style to suit your taste. Here, I have used metal hearts and simple white painted decorations. In the corner of a room, bang a nail in the beam and hang on the tree . . . if you cannot conveniently find anything to hang it from, then perhaps best to stick to the traditional tree, rather than wreck the house.

The most beautiful shape is the circle, it has no beginning, no end, and no middle. It's like the seasons, it goes round and round. I have illustrated here a selection of simple ideas which are self explanatory. Just have fun and experiment – they are easy to make. Let your imagination flow.

Rings, Wreaths, Hearts and Stuff

Simple Sprays

Collect 3 or 4 pieces of weeping birch, approx 1 m long. Group together and secure with string at the base. Cover kitchen table with old paper, we do everything on our kitchen table ... one old visitor to Carr Head told me she remembered someone having their tonsils out on the very same table ... Science has moved on, our table hasn't. As it might make a bit of mess you may prefer to do this outside. Get some old emulsion paint, I have used white in the illustration, just 'daub' a bit of paint here and there. It's a lovely job to do with kids in their 'old clothes'; it makes a very simple wall or ceiling decoration. I hang them on the beams and spread the branches about and tie up with fishing thread so visitors don't get a twig in the eye. Either leave plain or add simple shaker decorations.

If you are lucky enough to have one, take 3 sprays of contorted hazel; or be able to pinch a few branches from a friend. Just place in a very large container with a narrow neck and decorate with seasonal gifts. I love to do this in Church with Easter eggs it looks most effective on top of the font. I now have a very large collection of 'eggs' some are old and very fragile.

My neighbour Carol has geese and she gave me about eight eggs to make the Simnel cakes for Church; I very stupidly decided to make two holes in and blow. Having visited the doctors it was decided I hadn't got lock jaw or rapid gum disease and my cheeks weren't permanently damaged. The moral of the story is ... Don't try to blow goose eggs.

The Present Game

Now every time we have a family meal or friends at the table the boys always say 'please Granny can we play the pressie game'; they love it. It means you have to have a constant supply of presents. The most sought after presents of all are the beautiful, decorative trees that Michael and the boys make; they can never make enough. The instructions to make these wooden trees are on page 100.

Ingredients

A good mix of family or friends of any age (one person needs to be the dealer and the rest are the players)

Simple, little wrapped presents i.e. apples, oranges, soaps, chutneys, chocolates, teatowels, dusters or silly things (each person needs to bring a couple of pressies each)

2 packs of playing cards

Method

- First clear the table of all breakables and candles. It can get hectic as children do get excited when winning but beware of tears when they lose.
- Place all the presents in the centre of the table.
- The dealer keeps one pack of cards and deals out the other pack of cards to the players.
- The dealer then calls out the first card from their pack and the player who has the matching card gets to select a present from the centre of the table. This carries on until all the presents have been claimed.
- Then the game gets a bit more competitive; when the next player's card is called they get to take a present from somebody else.
- The game is over when the dealer has called out all the cards and then the presents sitting in front of you are yours to keep.

Coronation Chicken (Granny Mary's version)

Many times I get asked about Coronation Chicken, I make it so often in the summer but it's not my recipe, it originated in 1953 for the Queen's Coronation it was devised by the Women's Institute, the good old W.I. It was meant to be made the day before so everyone had the day off from the kitchen to enjoy the celebrations and watch television, if you were lucky enough to have one, or go to a friend's, otherwise the local village hall.

Ingredients

4	large chicken breasts
1 oz (25g)	butter
2	sweet onions peeled and chopped
2 tbs	curry powder (recipe on page 111)
1/2 pint (300ml)	good chicken stock or white wine
1	bay leaf, sage, and thyme or 1 tbs of dried mixed herbs
Juice of 1 lemon	
1/2 jar	apricot jam
1/2 pint (300ml)	mayonnaise
1/4 pint (150ml)	fresh whipped cream or Greek yoghurt
Salt and pepper	

Method

- In a pan, simmer the chicken breasts and the herbs in the stock or wine for 15 to 20 minutes until just cooked (not pink). Leave to cool in a bowl.
- Melt the butter in a pan, add the onions and cook until softened and golden – takes abot 5 mins. Next add the curry powder, lemon juice, apricot jam and simmer for a further 5 minutes. Allow to cool.
- Now whip the cream, and gently fold in the mayonnaise.
- Combine the sauce with the creams, and season.
- Cut the cooked chicken breasts into bite sized pieces and place in a large bowl. Add the sauce and stir in well. Double cover with cling film and place in the fridge.
- In order for the chicken to absorb all the flavours, it needs to be stirred form time to time. This dish is best made a day or two before required.

I've recently talked to my friends about what they remember about Coronation Day – nobody remembers having Coronation Chicken – maybe it was for the toffs with the teles. They all seem to think that we had chicken sandwiches, egg sandwiches and fancy buns. When I showed them my Coronation Spoon then instantly they remembered being presented with one, but where or by whom we can't remember, because we are now the Diamond Oldies.

I made this recently for a charity event in the village, and have included it because many who attended put in a request for the recipe. Because I am allergic to garlic, I cannot buy commercial curry powder, so after a bit of research and a lot of experimentation my grandson, Charlie, has become an expert at blending special spice mixes for me. For this event we used 80 chicken breasts, so he had to make a rather large amount. Since then he has had requests for jars of his special blend, so I have decided to include this too.

Jubilee Chicken

Here is another chicken dish of ours similar to Coronation Chicken. We devised it for my daughter Kim's wedding and originally called it Celebration Chicken, but I've now called it Jubilee Chicken in anticipation of the summer parties in 2012 to celebrate the Queen's Diamond Jubilee year.

Ingredients

8   free range chicken breasts

2   sweet onion sliced

     salt and pepper

     pinch grated nutmeg

½ pint (284mls)water/milk or white wine

2   limes

     Dozen dried apricots

1   small piece of freshly grated ginger

     fresh parsley and coriander

300gm   crème fraiche

300gm   Orzo – rice shaped pasta – good stuff!

6 large tbs   mayonnaise

2 tbs   fresh roasted almonds

creative decorations

Method

- Gently poach chicken breasts in chosen liquid (white wine is best) with sliced onion; add salt, pepper and nutmeg. Cook for 15 – 20 minutes, don't overcook because it will be dry and we don't want that do we, nor do we want it under cooked so check it's not pink – use a meat thermometer if you're not sure.
- Meanwhile grate a piece of ginger about 1" – 2" long, grate zest from limes and extract juices, cut apricots in half and chop parsley and coriander.
- When the chicken is cold cut into bite size cubes and stir in the above ingredients; make sure it's mixed well.
- Mix crème fraiche and mayonnaise together in another bowl then stir into the chicken mix.
- Double cover with cling film and place in fridge for at least a day for all the flavours to infuse.
- Stir from time to time.

It makes a good party dish served with rice salad and creative decoration; nasturtium flowers and edible petals, colourful fruits – mango, grapes, exotic stuff. I suppose cucumber if you must. See picture opposite for decoration suggestions.

Next Generation Stuff

Further Celebrations

Our Celebration Chicken was made with 50 chicken breasts for my daughter Kim's wedding. She had kindly given us all of six weeks notice, with a guest list of 175 and everything was to be homemade. Thankfully our dear friends were truly amazing in rallying round to help. Vats of carrot and coriander soup were made by one, and another made all the breads and was maître d' on the day with her team of ladies. We cooked 10 Salmon Wellington and there was also vegetarian lasagne, and makers of salads, salads and more salads. A dear friend made pecan pies to die for and over a two week period 250 meringues were prepared as well as several Bakewell puddings, and the cream was whipped in relays. We had teams of shoppers, runners, carriers and tasters, and others who decorated the tent and stable.

Michael, as always, was on hand to do those jobs that suddenly present themselves unexpectedly – he continually had a screwdriver in his pocket and a hammer in his hand. I remember running out of water at some stage and the power went off several times. We worked eighteen hour days, and looking back now I don't know how we did it. All the tables and chairs we could find in the village were collected by another friend who also helped Michael to lay yards of electric cable and kept us amused with his stories. Another who was handy with a camera was appointed our 'official photographer' for the big day but he wanted another job, so I told him to make and paint a sign for the 'pub' in the bottom stable. It was to be the 'Plum Tree and Mangle' but he got his trees mixed up and it ended up being 'The Pear Tree and Mangle' – which is as it remains in place to this day.

Our future son-in-law pulled in a lot of favours and soon china, cutlery, glass, music and a band were in place, and his parents made the best wedding cake I have ever tasted – it was divine, moist and rich.

It was a totally homemade 'do' and quite some achievement – I felt really proud. You're only as good as your friends, and our friends pulled out all the stops. I shall never forget their love and kindness on that special day; friends, family, teamwork.

What did I get out of it? I gained a wonderful son-in-law and later two very special grandsons to join the two granddaughters I already had. The boys are both 'foodies' and have always loved cooking, just as my son Peter did when he was a child a generation before. We spend a lot of fun time with the boys in the kitchen and you'll find recipes from both of them on the following pages. So hence I became Granny Mary and found my raison d'être.

Daughter Kim removing stubborn livestock from the house on the morning of her wedding, and the old 'Pear Tree and Mangle'.

Charlie's Stuff

Charlie's Curry Powder

Ingredients

8 tsp coriander

4 tsp cumin

2 tsp turmeric

1 tsp ground ginger

1/2 tsp chilli powder

1/2 tsp fenugreek

1/2 tsp allspice

1/4 tsp cinnamon

Method

Mix all the ingredients together in a bowl, and put into a suitable screw top jar until required.

Sausage and Bacon Quartet

Ingredients

1lb (455g)	pastry quantity
2lb (910g)	sausage meat
8 rashers	smoked streaky bacon cut into bits
2 large	onions peeled, sliced and gently fried in 2 tbs of oil
1tbs each	chopped fresh parsley, fresh sage (or dried)
	salt and pepper to taste
1	egg and a little milk to make a wash
2	peeled and sliced apples (optional)

Method

- Make the lb quantity of Granny's pastry (or buy from the shops) and rest (no don't you rest I meant rest the pastry) while you prepare the filling.

- Mix together sausage meat, bacon, cooked onions, chopped herbs, salt and pepper and apples if you like. I recommend the apple it gives a nice moist texture and just a little flavour (after all when you have roast pork you usually have apple sauce, so this is why we thought it would be a good idea).

- Roll out pastry to shape required. Now the idea is to put an amount of the filling in the middle of the rolled out pastry. Egg wash sides and bring together.

- We quartered the pastry and the filling to make 4 different shapes square, oblong, round etc. and finished with 6 small parcels, just an idea.

- Egg wash the tops, put into preheated over 210C (410F, Gas 7) for 15 minutes, turn down to 180C (360F, Gas 5) for a further 15 – 20 minutes till lovely and golden brown on top, cool on tray or eat straight away with friends – awesome.

Charlie's Bilberry or Blackberry and Apple pie

Bilberry Pie

First pick you bilberries; we are very lucky they grow wild round the back of the house and up on the moors. Every time I go out for a walk with the dogs in late summer Granny says "have you got a bag", its blackberries, bilberries or mushrooms, she doesn't mind what we come back with they all get used. Bilberry picking is especially tedious sometimes you only get a few and it takes four walks to collect enough to make a worthwhile pie.

Ingredients

1lb (455g)	bilberries (fresh if you are lucky or you can buy a jar), or stewed apple and blackberry.
	sugar to taste and sprinkle
8oz (225g)	pastry of your choice
	cream or custard

Method

- Pick over the fruit and put to one side.
- Roll pastry out and line bottom of dish. Put fruit into the lined dish with sugar on top.
- Roll remaining pastry to cover top, make a pattern round the edge.
- Egg wash and bake for 35 minutes approximately in hot oven until golden brown.
- Sprinkle caster sugar on top and serve with thick cream or homemade custard or both.

We use an old traditional tin or it may be enamel; it's a bit deeper than a plate 8" – 9". (20 – 23 cms).

Also Crumble

Ingredients

6oz (170g)	flour
4oz (115g)	butter
3oz (85g)	Demerara sugar
2 large tbs	ground almonds

Method

- Put flour into bowl, rub in butter to resemble fine breadcrumbs, add sugar and ground almonds if using.
- Put fruit in bowl or deep dish and put crumble on top, bake for 35 minutes in hot oven.

This got me into trouble; a lesson I shall never forget.

I made it for a take-and-share supper at friends. It was just about to be dished up when I said it had got a secret ingredient in it. Simon asked was there nuts in it – oh dear; he has a nut allergy; a very important lesson to learn.

Fraser's Stuff

Cheese and Vegetable Pies or Tarts

Ingredients

1lb	quantity of flaky pastry
Pk	Red Leicester grated
Pk	Cheddar grated
1 large	onion peeled, sliced and softened in butter
2 or 3	tomatoes cooked for a few minutes in butter
1	red pepper de-seeded and chopped and cooked in butter
Bag	spinach wilted in pan with butter
	salt and pepper
	sprinkling of mixed herbs
	butter to fry
	egg wash

Method

- Roll out the pastry first; I made a pie in a 1lb pork pie tin I was shown how to do it, rather like making a clay pot. Work it from the bottom up the sides.
- Next the more exciting bit, start the layers with Red Leicester then onion then tomato then Cheddar then spinach, sprinkle a few herbs in the middle and a little salt and pepper, do same again but next time put in red pepper instead of tomato till you've filled it to the top. You have to push down. Press it very well.
- Egg wash the top (egg wash means beat 1 egg and a little milk or water together, you need a pastry brush).
- Then you put the top on; roll pastry out to fit, squeeze edges and make a pattern and egg wash the top.
- Bake in hot oven. I used a timer for 30 minutes then looked; it needed about 15 minutes longer with oven turned down.

Banana Monkey Bars

Ingredients

8oz (225g)	butter
4oz (115g)	runny honey
4oz (115g)	soft brown sugar of light muscovado
14oz (400g)	porridge oats
10oz (285g)	any dried fruits you like (I like sour cherries)
1	orange rind
1	lemon rind
10oz (285g)	mixed chopped nuts
2	ripe mashed bananas

Method

- Grease a baking tray. Pre heat oven to 160C (310F, Gas 3).
- Put honey, butter and sugar in a large saucepan over a low heat. Stir from time to time until it's melted.
- Take off the heat and mix in oats, fruits, rind, nuts and lastly combine bananas.
- Place in baking tray and cook for 30 minutes until golden brown.
- Let it cool in the tin.
- Cut into fingers with a sharp knife (No don't cut your finger) maybe you should make squares.
- Store in an airtight tin or give away.

Our resident biscuit taster

Fraser is working to perfect the
perfect chocolate confection which
will of course feature in the next book!

Animal Stuff

Having spent all my life in close proximity to animals, both the farm and domestic type, it is not surprising that I have a soft spot for them. Sadly, they can never live as long as we do and there have been many tearful goodbyes we have had to endure over the years; pet lambs, cats and our dogs in particular have played an intrinsic part in our lives, and even after they have departed to the big doggy heaven there is always a part of them still with you, and which never goes away.

We Have A Secret

We have a secret, you and I
that no one else shall know,
for who but I can see you lie
each night in fire glow?

And who but I can reach my hand
before we go to bed
and feel the living warmth of you
and touch your silken head?

And only I walk moorland paths
and see ahead of me,
your small form racing with the wind
so young again, and free.

And only I can see you swim
in every brook I pass
and when I call, no one but I
can see the bending grass.

Anon

Photo by Rachel